Acknowledgment

I0485786

I would like to thank my darling wife Niamh for being everything I wanted in life.

To my children Kate and Rachel, you mean the world to me and you have made me realise what life is all about. You fill me full of giggles and joy every day.

Thanks for your help and understanding during the writing of this book.

This book is for the three of you

Preface

In 1994 I worked for two weeks in my father's companies head office as part of a work experience program in secondary school. My father had a big office which he shared with a colleague. At that time I thought this is where I want to work when I'm older. A big office, a nice view and enough room to practice the golf swing without interruption. Sure what more could you want? Fast forward to 2002 when I entered the professional working office, everything had changed. No longer were people working in large offices but instead big open plan spaces where everyone could see exactly what everyone else was doing. The big closed offices were only for the elite, the senior executives and high flyers. My dreams had been dashed and what I entered into was far removed to what I had experienced back in the spring of 1994.

What I set out to do with this book was to give a feel as to what the modern office is like and entails. It may not have been what I dreamt it to be when I was fourteen years old. Instead it has evolved rapidly in the last thirteen years since I started working. The first two chapters delve into the many facets and occurrences we now see daily on the office floor. I discuss the internal office, what I have seen in the last few years and the structure of work that seems to embody the modern organisation and office. I take a critical look at areas like recruitment and human resource management and question what they bring to the modern day office. Some of my opinions are polemical by nature but I do this on purpose so that you the reader will think hard about your recent experiences in work

From there I move on to a more light hearted approach and discuss the area of management speak. For those of you who work outside an office or haven't begun working professionally yet the phrases outlined in chapter two will appear strange but the reality is these phrases form part of the modern office floor. The majority of the phrases discussed are meaningless outside the sedentary office environment but inside the office walls they form a powerful and unbreakable hold on individuals who constantly use them.

What the final three chapters set out to achieve is to discuss areas that some might feel are taboo and taken for granted. Workplace bullying has become a scourge of the modern office and its increasingly negative effects are beginning to scar individuals and companies alike. I have experienced bullying first hand and I discuss my story as honestly and openly as possible. I hope my story evokes a powerful debate in your head as to whether bullying is a real problem in the workplace. We all work for various reasons but whether we like it or not the reality is money is the primary driver. Mortgages, bills, childcare fees, educational fees and so on need to be paid on a monthly basis.

With recent global financial events such as the recession taking a strong hold on individuals' daily lives I write about the pension problem facing Ireland and to a lesser extent the rest of the world.

From my past experience of working in the pension industry I try in simple terms to write about how underfunded our individual and company pension funds are and what can be done to rectify this matter. A pension's time-bomb has been ticking for the last twenty years and will keep ticking indefinitely if nothing is done about this fundamental issue. With an ageing population in Ireland the country faces a serious crisis in thirty years' time (when I myself will be a pensioner) of how to fund peoples pensions. The state will be overburdened with other costs and private pensions as is stands will be miniscule for the majority of workers. Public sector pensions whilst funded by the government and the taxpayer might not fare much better.

Finally I take a look at social media and show how some companies have embraced it and some have not. I give a brief history of social media and discuss some ways by which it can improve your business using some famous companies as examples. Personally I would advocate the use of social media in every company as when used wisely it can benefit a company no end. The pitfalls need to be factored in but I explain that using social media should not hinder any businesses reputation once used properly. For an in-depth look at the area of social media and for any advice regarding this area please feel free to consult the following website thetalkingparrots.com.

To add further substance and clarity to the final three chapters I decided to draft a survey. The survey contained ten questions on office bullying, stress, pensions and social media usage. I sent the survey out to my LinkedIn connections which totalled approximately 600 in mid 2014. When the survey was closed in early 2015, 250 people had responded. The primary reason for sending this survey out was to get a feeling for how modern day workers felt on the topics I was discussing. Whilst the response rate falls short of the survey industry norm of 1000 respondents it does prove useful as the majority of respondents are working professionals. Its relative low numbers should not detract from its value.

As the book is written from my own perspective and experiences it could be argued it is a subjective exercise that may bear no resemblance to other individuals' experience. I let you the reader make this choice but I do hope that some of my experiences evoke some work memories of your own whether serious or humorous. Finally all I hope is that you read the book with an open mind and that it proves thought provoking and stimulating.

Enjoy.

David A Malone

August 2015

Index

Acknowledgments

Preface

Chapter 1

Chapter 2

Management Speak   **73**

Chapter 3

The Office Bully   **102**

Chapter 4

Pensions - A ticking time bomb!   156

Chapter 5

Social media in business   197

Chapter 1

The Modern Office –

Twenty things to look out for!

1. The Old vs the New Office

It's hard to put an exact time when the office went open plan but it dates back to the arrival of new and modern technologies namely e-mail and the internet. It's become more apparent from the late 1990s onwards. Work quickly became flexible, adaptable and transferable. Problems and information could be passed on within micro seconds via e-mail. The old style office where one or two people sat quietly in front of their computers locked away from the rest of the company were over.

Within a few small years the dynamics of the office had changed. This is not to say the old style didn't work, it worked perfectly well for years but technology and ultimately costs meant an open plan structure was more beneficial to organisations and employees. Less time was spent on the phone as e-mail became an easy way to contact colleagues internally and clients externally. Though this has gone full circle now as if you walk into any office you'll soon find that colleagues will just as quick pick up the phone to the person next to them than pop their head over the partition wall and say hello.

Whereas working in enclosed offices meant you could take regular breaks, put your feet up, read the paper or take a twenty minute snooze if you so desired, open plan offices are far less accommodating. You will get the feeling you are being watched or even spied upon and more often than not your senses will prove to be right. There will always be someone on the office floor who has little or next to little to be doing, that they will engage in checking up and snooping on other colleagues.

Privacy is definitely an issue with open plan offices but companies will argue that it sets everyone on a level playing field as only a few individuals have offices of their own which should mean there is less of an inferior complex amongst colleagues at work. Hoardings or partitions can give some privacy but when your manager is sitting right beside or behind you these have limited effect.

For college graduates who dreamt of having their large office and to be able to practice their golf swing, the chances are you will have to wait a while for this unless you get lucky and fast track your way through the ranks of a company. Or you could become your own boss. But remember you don't need CCTV in open plan offices as beware you are being watched. But like everything else in life you'll soon get used it, you won't have a choice.

2. Leadership, a quality thin on the ground

Leadership is a quality bestowed on many, but few rarely have the necessary qualities to lead. Many books and articles have been written on what qualities good leaders should have and what traits bad leaders have. For good leaders these are, charisma, delegation, ability to influence others, be knowledgeable, good communicator, decisive, confident, determined, proactive, adaptable, being a forward thinker and so on. For bad leaders traits can include being self absorbed, egotistical, manipulative, vindictive, poor communicator, reactive, incompetent, insular, obsessive, callous and so on. The main quality that I believe leaders should have is respect. They should command it and show it to their peers. Good leaders, no matter what walk of life they are in, either teachers, politicians, managers and even parents have to command respect or else they are deemed redundant in their field.

Two stories, one from my secondary school days and another from the modern day sporting arena show how leadership can be positive and also how it can corrode feelings and generate anger amongst people.

When I was in secondary school in Ireland back in the early to mid 1990s there was one teacher in the school that commanded total respect. He wasn't the principal or the vice principal; he was a Maths teacher and only stood a meagre 5.4. inches tall. The main reason I think he was respected by students and colleagues alike was because he was an excellent teacher who could get the best out of ordinary pupils. If you were late for his class after lunch he wouldn't let you in the door. No one was late as they didn't want to feel the wrath of this man. He called every pupil by their surnames, and even though I thought it a little strange at first; what it did do was give the pupils a sense of feeling more grown up in a teenager's world.

No other teacher in the school commanded respect of the pupils, not one. In fact nearly all got verbally abused and harassed on a daily basis by the pupils, yet my Maths teacher never got any abuse from pupils, no one would dare. Abuse of teachers was common in secondary school, so to escape this was unique.

His complete control and respect in the school was brought home one day when the students decided to have a protest at the cancellation of our annual sports day because of a lack of school board funding. The protest was held in sports pitches in the school grounds and over 200 pupils had a sit out and wouldn't go back to class after lunch. The principal marched down and demanded we return to class. Nothing happened, nobody moved. He was jeered and laughed at. No one took too much notice of him; he was arrogant and didn't have the authority needed for his position. Even threats of Saturday morning detention and suspension didn't deter the students in their protests. Next to come down was the vice-principal. He was feared a little more but was also seen as a joker. The problem he had is that he engaged too much with pupils and this corroded the respect they had for him. A fine balance was needed here.

None of the students were moving and over thirty minutes had elapsed. Then like a gust of wind from a hurricane the Maths teacher marched down the field. The students at the front shouted, *"shit it's the Maths teacher, run"*. To this day I've never seen a group of 200 people move as quick. We all rushed back into class. I was only fourteen and didn't have this man as a teacher so I wasn't too sure of his reputation. But I soon learned he was the most respected and feared man in the school. The reason, well there could be many. The obvious one was that there was always a good chance that he would be your teacher at some stage. I had him for two years at senior cycle. He was easily the best teacher in the school, I never learned as much from any other teacher. He didn't take any nonsense and crap from students and other teachers. He was his own man; he did it his way and didn't let anyone interfere in his teaching.

He would quickly put you in your place if you stepped out of line or answered him back. That was one thing you wouldn't dare do. He wasn't scared to stand up to any unruly student even if the days of corporal punishment were long gone. The respect he received was genuine. He was a principal in waiting but sadly this never came his way which was unfortunate as he had the qualities to be a fantastic principal. Possibly his isolation from senior teachers in the school prevented him getting the job, or maybe he just didn't want it.

So without doubt the two biggest qualities someone must have to be a good leader are to be excellent at what you do and to command respect from your peers and subordinates. And you can't forget you need to put a little bit of fear into your followers or in my teachers case, the pupils. Being arrogant will only antagonise people. Fear will keep the mind alert.

In sport great leadership is the difference between winning and losing. Look at all the battles Patrick Viera and Roy Keane had in the late 1990s and early 2000s in the FA English Premiership (football). Would Arsenal FC and Manchester United FC have won as many trophies without these players? The simple answer is no, but not just because they were fantastic footballers, it's because they had great leadership qualities and captained their teams by commanding respect and leading by example, same as Brian O'Driscoll for the Ireland rugby team and Martin Johnson for England rugby team during the Rugby World cup in 2003.

FIFA scandal – In 2011 high level officials in FIFA (football's governing body) were accused of offering and accepting money in exchange for votes in the organisations presidential election and in the world cup venue voting for 2018 and 2022. Russia and Qatar won the vote amidst great surprise from the world media and under a dark cloud of suspicion, bribes and backhanders. The UKs bid seemed the best, in fact there was no doubt it was but yet Russia won. Qatar's bid didn't make any sense, the heat in the summer months can be near 50c and no less than 40c, far too hot to play football, yet they won the vote. The integrity of the decisions to award the World Cups to these countries and ultimately the integrity of the FIFA President Sepp Blatter has come under question and scrutiny. Famed for his gaffs and non politically correct manner, Blatter's presidency has been one of intrigue and accusation.

FIFA demand that governments and the legal professions of countries don't interfere in the running of football, yet as an organisation themselves they lack openness and transparency.

Blatter constantly refutes all accusations of vote rigging, bribes and a dictatorship style running of FIFA. His credibility has all but disappeared and as he clings on to power for another few years, only a new leader with new ideas can help FIFA regain lost credibility and trust in the public's eye. The chances of that happening are slim, as new candidates with modern ideas are few and far between. Michel Platini who is currently the head of UEFA (Europe's governing football body) was seen as a future FIFA president in the waiting, but his lack of acceptance or willingness to experiment and embrace new technologies has put him out of touch with the modern day football fan. In mid 2014 Platini ruled himself out of the running for the FIFA Presidential contest in 2015. This left Blatter again as the front runner. Others such as David Ginola and Luis Figo put themselves forward but the result was a foregone conclusion with Blatter winning albeit by a smaller margin then he anticipated. Subsequently Blatter announced he was resigning and a new FIFA general election will now take place in February 2016. Blatter has stated he will definitely not run but only time will tell..

With the FIFA merry go round in full swing as of early August 2015 Platini announced he would run for FIFA president. His prime reason being that he is unlikely to face any real competition for the post. Some might argue that Platini would be a complete failure as President, but a change is needed in this organisation. FIFA as it stands seems an organisation against change and totally content with the status quo, even if this means that their reputation will continue to erode further amongst the discerning football fans globally (if that is possible at this stage).

Football after all is the world's most popular game, possibly because it's the easiest, most affordable and accessible to all.

When Blatter decided to investigate the allegations of bribes and misconduct in FIFA, he initially set up an ethics committee, which was entirely internally based. Not surprisingly he was cleared of any wrong doing. This process lacked any credibility and possibly as a result (and intense global media pressure) an independent enquiry was sanctioned by FIFA to be carried out by Michael J Garcia. When the report was finished FIFA refused to release its contents and Garcia resigned as FIFAs ethics investigator. Eventually in late 2014 after internal calls by Platini, numerous other FIFA delegates and the world media FIFA released the 430 page report. Their fight to keep the report away from the public eventually failed leaving the suspicion that they were trying to hide something all along. Unfortunately for FIFA their reputation has taken such huge hits in the last few years that it would take an amazing public relations representative and a complete overhaul of the organisation for the public to have any faith in it again. The current man at the helm Blatter seems oblivious to this fact and this along with other not so discerning qualities make him a poor leader and a liability as far as FIFAs global reputation is concerned. Such events as former FIFA president Joao Havelange being found guilty of bribery and misconduct has not helped either.

After the World Cup vote for the tournaments in 2018 and 2022 the General Secretary of FIFA, Frenchman Jerome Valcke said that Qatar had *"bought"* the vote. He quickly explained what he meant, saying that the bid was well financed, that's all. I wonder what you believe. In early 2015 the Daily Telegraph newspaper in England reported that primary sponsors, Castrol, Continental tyres and Johnson and Johnson had stopped their association with FIFA. The companies explained the decisions were made purely for business reasons but I suspect the negative publicity surrounding FIFA played a big part in their respective decisions. A British politician Damian Collins recently described FIFA as a toxic brand.

FIFA have become a law onto themselves but with reputation a key driver of success and public perception FIFAs leadership can in my opinion only be deemed a failure. In America the president can only be elected for consecutive terms, which means eight years in total. FIFA should consider a similar model and while it won't eradicate possible corruption or bad leadership it will make the organisation more democratic.

Giovanni Trappatoni - he was the Ireland football manager whose CV was spectacular yet his style of football and management was prehistoric and outdated. He had a philosophy and a rigid way of managing and playing that was not open to change even under great pressure and scrutiny to do so. He had his pride and was belligerent to the end.

But when the facts become glaringly obvious something must change. In September 2012 Ireland fluked their way to a 2-1 win against Kazakhstan (in a World Cup 2014 Qualifier) after being outplayed for 85 minutes by as poor a team as you might see in international football. A dubious penalty decision (and I'm Irish) in favour of Ireland started their escape which was finished off by an injury time goal. This performance and result in tandem with an appalling Euro 2012 tournament campaign should have meant at the very least questions had to be asked of the manager and what he was doing. Hard liners demanded he left and I tended to agree. He had plenty of chances to succeed, and at one level did reasonably well in qualifying Ireland for Euro 2012 (this can be qualified by Ireland being given a lucky play-off draw against Estonia, a team of lesser standing in European football).

My point and argument is that Trappatoni was a manager who lived off past glories and his failures were clear to see in a modern and forward thinking world. He should have gone before he was eventually pushed and sacked by the FAI. He had begun to alienate supporters with his belligerent refusal to change the style of play of the team. Football had moved on but his management style had not. And while I appreciate his reluctance to change what he perceived as a perfect model because of past glories, change had to be embraced if Ireland were not to fall even further behind in the global football rankings.

When this analogy is transferred to the corporate business world it is shown that managers can get lost in a fast paced changing global environment and rely too heavily on past performance and glories. I have worked in many Irish financial service companies, and some still to this day are stuck in a time warp using outdated technology platforms and employing managers who are way out of their depth and lack the basic management and communication skills to succeed. A lack of foresight, knowledge and forward thinking to do jobs competently is there for all to see. Bad leadership, or even a perception of, can be a recipe for disaster in any organisation and with reputation a key driver of profits this is not something that can be taken lightly.

3. Your wages might not go as far as you think

While to some people this will come as no surprise for others it will hit them like a train. When I began my professional career and entered the so called *"real world"* over a decade ago my living expenses and costs were minimal. The reason being I was living at home in my parents' house so I had no mortgage, no car loan, no bills or household expenses. Life was easy. I could socialise at the weekends free in the knowledge that I didn't have to worry how much money I was wasting. Nowadays it's different like most people I am over burdened with costs that range from car, household bills, crèche fees, educational costs, petrol, lunches and commuting costs, the list is endless.

With continuous recession and austerity based direct and indirect taxes implemented from the Irish government life has only got harder. The incentives to work are becoming less but the hard question is what else would we do to earn money or pass the time by without working. So unless the long established social and economic norms of society change, we will all have to survive in a much tougher and tightened working environment going forward.

Employers will expect increased knowledge and will work employees at minimum wages and some employment will verge on exploitation. To earn that extra euro or dollar will mean sacrifices. This could be simply working extra hours, but remember my motto has always been to never work for free. This is a bad habit to get into and if an employer knows you'll do it once, you are doomed as they will take it for granted that unpaid work is the norm. There is nothing more true than the old adage of *"time is money"*, so never waste your time and always get paid for it. Time is something you can never get back and always remember the difference between organisational and personal goals. Don't be too quick to get sucked into a culture of unpaid work in any organisation as ultimately it is the organisation that is benefiting from this and not you.

So some simple rules to enhance your earnings when you first start working or are a seasoned professional, always get paid for any work you do and don't be afraid to subsidise your main income with additional consultancy work if you have expert knowledge in certain areas whether they be niche or not. Examples here are information and communications technology consultancy or financial advice if a qualified accountant. Learn to save money from early on, it's hard but a rewarding habit to get into and beware of the rainy days when you'll need those extra few pennies you have put aside.

4. Contract vs Permanent roles

Ask yourself this question and answer it honestly. Would you prefer to be working in a permanent or contract based role? My guess is that the majority will answer they prefer the permanent job. It's a reasonable answer to give but contract work should not be dismissed out of hand. Since 2007 when the last global financial crisis begun contract work has become prevalent for the average worker with employers reluctant to commit to offering permanent work. Contract work offers many benefits including enhanced flexibility to move between jobs and also opportunities to experience different corporate cultures and build up valuable work experience that should progress your career.

My father worked in what would be called a pensionable job. To most modern day private sector workers this expression makes little or no sense. It simply doesn't exist anymore. While some people may think it does, believe me there is no such thing as a job for life

14

anymore. When my parents used hear I'm moving job they always seemed to be shocked and scared. I haven't lived at home for many years and I am married but because they grew up in a culture of "*a job for life*", the concept of having a career where you might change jobs frequently is alien to them.

So if you had the choice tomorrow of accepting a permanent position or a two year contract, which would you accept? It's a tough question and understandably the majority of people would accept the permanent job. But in times of job instability a permanent job is not really permanent. An employer could without warning decide that redundancies are needed to reduce the cost base. This is the chance we all take when working. However the two year contract or any contract should not be ruled out as it may be a viable option in your current circumstances. The likelihood is if a company is offering a one or two year contract that at a minimum it will last this long but invariably it should get extended if both parties agree on this.

But choosing the two year contract is wholly subjective and a decision like this needs to be made in the context of the prevailing economy and personal circumstances that exist at a particular period in time. We should remember contract work is still work and employers will at times compensate better for short term work, especially in niche and technically driven sectors like information technology. Obviously benefits packages are important when choosing a job and this is where permanent roles tend to outweigh contract roles. It can be assumed that permanent jobs will offer pensions, bonuses, health insurance, gym subscriptions, travel allowances and so on. Contract work is based predominantly on pure salary with little or no benefits attached. The salary may be higher but the difference in benefits packages can quickly erode the salary deficit. It is for the individual to choose which are the most valuable.

While there is no doubt that permanent jobs offer security especially in the public sector where getting fired is a non runner, don't be too quick to dismiss contract type roles. Career progression in contract roles can be real and some contract roles are made permanent after time. But what are the main benefits and disadvantages of working contract roles? Here are some to consider when choosing between contract and permanent job roles.

Advantages of contracts

- Freedom of movement, if you don't like the role
- You can just do your job, nothing more should be expected.
- You can work many contracts and experience different companies, environments and cultures whether good or bad
- You can build up vast experience quickly
- When moving jobs potential employers do not quiz you on why you are moving, as it should be obvious
- If you have specialised in a particular field it can work in your favour and you can command a good salary
- Shows you are flexible, adaptable and take new ideas on board quickly

Disadvantages

- There is a lack of job certainty and stability.
- You can find yourself out of work and might get screwed on salary.
- Might not experience the perks of permanent staff – pensions, bonuses, health insurance, etc.
- Career progression could suffer and stall.
- You can be treated less favourably than permanent staff
- Employers might exploit your position by demanding overtime is done, or else no contract extension. (this is only an issue if you want to extend your contract)
- It can be hard to move from contract to permanent roles as employers and recruitment agencies assume you want to continue doing contract only work.
- A perceived lack of continuity in your CV may hurt your prospects of landing a permanent role
- Internal opportunities tend to be limited to permanent employees
- *Zero hour contracts* - are becoming more popular and offer little security. Some view these contracts as exploiting workers but employees need to know that these contracts can mean no hours one week, five hours the next week and then intense bursts of long shifts when companies get busy. On-line retailers like amazon.com and sportsdirect.com use contracts like these. They are popular in the hotel and catering industry as well. Recent bad publicity regarding zero-hour contracts has led the Irish

government to research further into the area on how it is impacting the economy and employees. In April 2015 Dunnes Stores (a supermarket and clothing chain) employees in Ireland went on a days strike in protest against their terms of employment. One of their main gripes with the company was the use of zero-hour contracts which employees felt gave them no stability and hindered their ability to pay monthly bills including mortgages. The company has so far refused to negotiate with the employees on strike which has only meant the situation has become more volatile, with further strikes planned.

- *Fixed term contracts* – there is no certainty that they will be extended and tend not to come with the perks of permanent contracts such as pension entitlements and health benefits. They work similar to permanent roles in that you work nine to five and are expected to do the same work as if you were permanent but extensions are uncertain. In some jurisdictions fixed rate contracts have to be made permanent after a set period. In Ireland this is four years. In a previous job I worked on a fixed term contract basis. My contract was renewed annually for two years (so renewed after year one and two, totalling a three year stay) but when it came to renewing for the third time (fourth year) it was terminated. The company were well within their rights not to extend the contract. However my suspicions are it was not extended due to the fact that under Irish law they would have had to make me permanent with an extra year's extension. This could have cost the company a lot of money in extra benefits which possibly in a recession they were unwilling to give.

- *Daily rate contracts* – these are sold on the basis of receiving a set wage for each day you work which tends to be higher than a permanent salary on offer for the same role. However this extra money is watered down by the fact that you receive no payment for sick-days or holiday leave. Also there is an obligation on the employee to pay social insurance not the employer and if the employer so chooses they can terminate your contract with immediate effect with no payment of a months' notice in advance. So unlike fixed term contracts you would receive no payment of a months' notice. This makes day rate contracts very dangerous. For some employees it is the money that dictates their choice. You also need to bear in mind that the company you are working in is technically not your employer. You are self-employed and will need to look after your own tax and payroll affairs yourself. The alternative is paying a management company a set fee normally between €100 and €150 a month to look after this. This is very expensive over one calendar year, another negative side to day rate contracts. One previous recruitment agency said to me that a €55,000 salary in a permanent role would be equivalent to €350 a day on a daily rate contact. The daily rate contact could earn you €80,000 if you worked every day but when benefits lost, sick leave and other unforeseen events are factored in the €80,000 begins to dwindle fast.

5. Red Pen City

This is a crèche/playschool way of managing colleagues. It simply doesn't work and only angers and frustrates employees. The *"Red Pen City"* concept is one I came up with myself. It describes a manager who will review employees work and cover draft reports in red pen, even if the mistakes that have been made are minimal and are of no consequence. By definition the *"Red Pen City"* type manager is pedantic and anal by nature. Corrections are normally highly subjective from the manager's point of view and the red ink is used to show who is in control and has the power.

Red by definition is a colour of rage and anger and managers are indirectly showing subordinates that they are in charge and control the way reports should be completed. It's the do it my way or the high way approach. I worked for a manager in the past that loved to micro-manage and loved red biros. A combination made in heaven for my manager at the time, but not for me. On numerous occasions I would complete a report, check it and be confident there was little or no mistakes in it and if there was, the mistakes were of a cosmetic nature or subjective from the point of view of the reviewer.

Without fail on every occasion I would receive a report back covered in red pen to the point where I was nearly going blind looking at it. This particular manager's style made employees feel like primary school pupils and she was the teacher. I don't think the manager had grasped that we were working in a professional organisation and I had over ten years experience doing what I was doing and was proficient at it. When I questioned why there was so much red pen on the pages I was swiftly rebuked and told to make the corrections immediately. It was like working under a dictator.

Making the corrections did not benefit anyone except herself. There was no value to me or the company and I certainly wasn't learning anything. This approach to management is childlike and it lacks the basic skills that all managers should have, that colleagues should be treated with respect.

This style of management is akin to an audit mentality of too much *"ticking and bashing"*, overkill in checks and being a perfectionist. From my experience it is primarily a trait of managers lacking in self confidence and good communication skills. It can be very frustrating to deal with. The main problems associated with the *"Red Pen City"* approach are;

- It alienates people
- It causes rifts between colleagues
- Produces unnecessary workloads and overtime
- It adds no value to work processes
- Produces pedantic and anal staff that can damage relations with external and internal stakeholders
- Employees don't see the big picture
- Staff get bogged down in small mundane, worthless and no value adding tasks.

- It causes contempt and resentment of colleagues and managers
- It makes for a bad working culture and environment

6. Learn to be diplomatic and take criticism

There are many thousands of management consultants working today but if you were to learn one thing they had to say it would be always be diplomatic and take criticism even if it's the biggest pile of nonsense you've ever heard. Suck it up as even with poor and badly delivered criticism you will learn something. Constructive criticism in any job is welcome and beneficial once it is delivered in a professional and objective manner. Numerous managers in today's business world lack soft skills and tend to get personal and highly subjective when delivering criticism. Never be tempted into responding in an abusive and derogatory way, this will only show you in a poor light but will give the manager who is delivering the review greater satisfaction.

When I started my first job out of college, I was professionally very green and if I'm being honest quite immature. I didn't respect management and authority and at times showed contempt. I was too headstrong and thought managers were out to have a go at me when in reality the majority of them were trying to improve my communication and business skills. At the time I couldn't see this and it has taken over ten years for me to be able to see a good manager who is trying to give valuable constructive criticism as opposed to a poor manager who lacks basic communication skills and whose criticism is delivered in a subjective and self fulfilling way.

Below is a short story from my days in my first job, not something I'm proud of but a story that will benefit workers out there who are thinking of confronting a manager or who tend to react and get provoked easily. It is a prime example of how not to behave. It was my first job, I was eager and keen to impress but the learning curve I had expected had not materialised.

On the job training was a new experience and getting used to office politics and clicks (groups of workers who socialised together internally) was proving difficult. Three months passed and I was beginning to think I had made a mistake and a new career direction was in order even this early. I decided I was going to leave, but was talked out of this my one of the senior managers. In fact she was leaving the company but I didn't know this at the time. I put my head down and tried to make the best impression I could and worked hard. Another three months passed and it was time for my interim appraisal or performance review. I was genuinely expecting a good review and as I had never been through the experience of reviews of this nature before I wasn't sure what to expect.

The operations manager conducted the review and started off my going through areas of weakness that I needed to improve on. It seemed to be going on forever and I could feel myself getting angry, and the frustration was beginning to build. Was there no good points to talk about, there was but I was impatient. At this early stage in my professional career I was not good at dealing with constructive criticism or any type of criticism for that matter. Any form of criticism directed at myself was like waving a red flag to a bull. All of sudden I began giving back chat to the operations manager and before I could stop myself I uttered an a expletive in his direction and in no uncertain terms told him where to go. When most people would have apologised I continued my tirade of verbal abuse towards him. I stormed out of the meeting room shouting on the way. It was close to 5pm and I went straight home.

When the dust settled and I went back into work the next day I was expecting a phone call by HR or the operations manager himself. None came. The company was well within their rights to fire me, as what I had done was shameful. A written warning at least, surely was coming. The whole incident was left to blow over without retribution. To this day I am not sure why they deemed fit not to reprimand me. The only reasoning I could think of was that I was a novice, green and lacking in any professional communication. I have great respect for the operations manager even if I never showed it. The way he handled the situation was admirable as most individuals would have probably used their power to sack me on the spot. This little story is one about how not to behave and to learn to bite your lip when been given criticism that you might not agree with. I certainly learnt a great deal from it and it was the starting point in my personal professional development.

On the other hand it showed a professional and sensitive side to management. Not many managers out there would have left that go, but to the credit of the operations manager, he brushed it under the carpet and put it down to experience. It would have been easy and very tempting to sack me, but he showed great character and foresight. Maybe he wanted to see me develop, who knows? But he definitely showed a touch of class that day, something regretfully I didn't do.

7. Training, what training – It's a sink or swim culture in today's business world!

You wouldn't expect Apple or Microsoft not to invest in research and development throughout their business; this would not make any sense. How would they develop the iPhone or next fad that will have customers queuing for days to get their hands on it? You would think therefore that companies in general would invest in people development and to be specific, training. Richard Branson, famed entrepreneur and founder of the Virgin Group is accredited with saying *"train people well enough so they can leave; treat them well enough so they don't want to"*. The above quote might be construed that training has a double edged sword effect in that if you train employees well they will leave, but if you don't train them at all they will leave too. But what Branson is trying to say in my opinion is that good training is part of treating staff well and if we do this they won't want to leave in the first place. Therefore it is a necessity not a luxury.

I've worked for over thirteen years and in many different organisations, but I have yet to be part of a training or induction program that I derived any benefit out of. In fact most companies operate an on the job type training program where you sit with a co-worker or just learn as you go. This is done for many reasons but the primary one is to save costs. But if companies were more forward thinking and truly employee oriented they would and should invest in training.

The consequences of not investing are stark. Employees can soon become disillusioned with their role, if they feel they have not been trained in properly. This can lead to resentment towards their managers and the job itself; ultimately meaning they might not see a potential viable career path in that particular organisation. When this happens staff turnover becomes a real and relevant issue.

When I was studying for my primary Degree in Business Management I looked at numerous case studies of how well managed and run businesses were in Japan and America. It was seldom I came across a case study that referred to a business in Ireland, but that could have been because the books I studied were driven at an American market, or it could simply have been that back in the late 1990s it was hard to find a business in Ireland that embraced training and development of their staff.

When I came out of college I had high expectations that any company I joined would have an interesting and interactive training program that would settle me in to the job and make me relate to colleagues within the organisation quicker. Unfortunately the longest induction program I have ever been on lasted one half day and the majority of the course was taken up by self promoting the company, a form of propaganda you might say. I found that if induction courses were not conducted properly they were a pure waste of time. I was left to rot in one company for the first two weeks reading health and safety manuals and company policies. I had no systems access and no e-mail; it was so boring and frustrating that I considered leaving and finding a new job. I didn't leave, I still am not sure why and ended up staying for nearly two years, but I did think to myself there will be individuals in the future who won't put up with that. The first few weeks and months in any job are critical for an employee to settle in and an inclusive training program can help here.

Everyone has worked in one, two or maybe more jobs where training is non-existent. In fact it seems to be the norm in more and more companies, the culture of sink or swim is there for all to see. Starting any new job is stressful and a daunting experience even for more mature business professionals. Being introduced to your team and colleagues you will be working with would help, but I'm afraid in some companies it is too much to ask for and simply won't happen. It's not because your colleagues don't like you, it's simply that they more often than not don't care and don't have the time. It's up to you to introduce yourself to new staff members and embrace the new culture. The upshot for me was that I found this improved my soft skills within the work place. I had no choice I had to become more confident and proactive in phoning and meeting new faces.

Since 2007 the world global marketplace has been in turmoil which has meant a contracted jobs market and the rise of temporary contract type work. This in itself has lead to companies cutting costs to increase or stabilise profits. Easy targets are redundancies but training is not too far behind. In essence this is a false profit, as what you invest in people you will get back two fold and more. Don't invest in them and they will leave and the cost to replace experienced staff with valuable sensitive tacit knowledge is high. But don't be fooled into thinking that organisations will listen to this argument, they won't.

The question is - what is the best way to treat new staff members when they join a modern organisation? James Caan CBE, of Dragons Den UK fame is a successful business man with decades of experience. In one of his many LinkedIn pieces he talks about his approach to new staff. This approach which I find difficult to fault is to let the new employee gradually settle in to the job and not to expect someone to hit the ground running straightaway. This will take two to three months which is a reasonable timeframe. The critical point raised by Caan is that you can't let any future employee left to their own devices when they start; you need to have a structured induction program in place that is tailored to their needs. This should be the responsibility of their manager, no matter what section of the business they are in. The job description should be mapped out with a list given showing all of the employees internally that the person is liable to come into contact with within the course of their day to day job. Small introductory meetings should be organised with each individual to make them feel at ease almost immediately. As mentioned starting any new job brings anxiety, so if this can be reduced then that's a great start.

Even meetings with receptionists, facilities and post room colleagues are part of the process as this endears the new employees further to the core values and ethics that operate within the organisation. Long winded presentations and meetings are not recommended by Caan. Instead he favours one to one meetings with new managers and colleagues where questions on roles and objectives can be freely discussed. The main point which is hard to argue with is that the more you invest in an induction process the quicker an employee feels at home and ultimately the company will reap the benefits through increased productivity. It's not rocket science, invest in new starters through training, communication and development and you are likelier to have a happier employee who will on average stay longer within the organisation, not only to the benefit of the employee but the organisation as a whole. The sooner businesses see this, then the sooner their business grows and succeeds in an increasingly competitive global environment.

To the modern worker lack of investment in training is commonplace, we just get on with our jobs, and it's what we expect. To the future graduate embarking on a new career, don't be too disappointed in the induction program you end up on, look on the bright side, its more than some other people get, who don't get trained at all.

8. Don't always believe the job description

The first rule is don't always believe what's in the job description. Some are flowered and glossed up to increase interest in mundane and boring jobs. At least 50%, if not more, of what you will actually be doing in a job will not be in the job description. If it was fewer candidates would apply for the job advertised.

From my own experience I have been promised the star, sun and moon in job descriptions and interviews but when it came to starting a new job I found out it was all lies. In one particular job I worked I spend 50% of my time doing jobs such as opening post, updating post log spreadsheets, writing and lodging cheques, archiving, and unbelievably emptying and filling up the dishwasher as the company was too mean to hire a cleaner to do this. I had over ten years experience yet these were the jobs I was spending my time doing and of course these were not listed in the job description. If they had of been I would never have applied for the position, in fact a school drop-out might not even have applied for the job. Deceiving potential candidates like this is not illegal but it's definitely immoral and not the way for a modern day company to conduct business. The problem here is you can't go asking in an interview what *"crap"* jobs if any you are going to be doing if you accept this role. If you go down this road or line of questioning then no job offer will come in the first place. It's a catch 22 position as you don't want to find yourself one month into a new job and find your daily task list being of a level that shows contempt to your skill set. There is no point being naive and thinking this doesn't happen, the sad reality is it does and can be quite common. Don't get me wrong we all have to do some boring and routine tasks, but I would prefer if companies were honest from the start of the hiring process and detailed the job description accurately with no hidden agenda. This puts everyone on a level playing field.

The recession and global financial crisis has meant companies have begun to force staff to do the job of others. More administration type work has become the norm in many positions. The reasoning is that companies don't want to pay administrators to do the job; instead they merge what would be part of their job in to yours.

My advice is to be extremely careful when accepting a role at a low to medium level (senior and executive type roles should in theory escape the mundane, sole destroying tasks). Do some research and if you know someone working for the company get all the information you can about the department you might potentially be working in. Recruitment agencies if they are worth their salt should be able to give you a good briefing of the team and company you are going into, but ultimately they are a client of the company so they will always gloss companies up to be something they may not be.

Take time to decide on a job offer, ask the company if they will give you a tour of the office, (most will decline but no harm in asking) and importantly don't let a recruitment agency force you into taking a position, remember they are on commission. You need to make the right choice for yourself, but the uncontrollable factor here is that you will never know what a company is really like until you work for them, and that is the chance we all have to take.

9. Deadlines, deadlines and more deadlines

Unfortunately we live in a business world that is primarily profit driven but with that comes enhanced time pressures. These pressures can intensify in our day to day lives to such an extent that they drive us to feelings of heightened stress and anxiety. My experience of working over the last thirteen years tells me that the majority of businesses nowadays are so client and cost driven that deadlines have to be achieved no matter what the underlying circumstances are. This can mean overtime, weekend work, highly stressed environments and fundamentality bad corporate cultures in the workplace. Frequently I am being told by managers that it is imperative, crucial, critical and vital that certain reports are finished on time. Not all things are imperative or critical; we all just fall into the trap of believing this.

If we take a step back and think to ourselves, do all deadlines need to be met on time, or are we just putting our staff under incredible pressure to gain those extra few Dollars or Euros. I've worked in numerous companies with some more flexible than others but all without fail are time and money driven. If a client says jump, invariably companies say how high. I'm not sure if this is the ideal way to run businesses, it might mean higher turnover in monetary terms but it could also mean higher turnover in staffing terms as highly stressed workers will tend to move job, if not in the short term, definitely in the mid to long term.

I spent nearly five years working in the funds industry, notorious for constant deadlines and late working hours. Quite simply it's a young man's game and something I got out of before I was thirty years old. Whilst I never conformed to the overtime culture in funds companies, the deadlines were unavoidable and highly pressurised. Some clients wanted unrealistic turnarounds on their reporting, which forced employees to work under unnecessary pressure. But with money to be made in a competitive environment, companies were to glad to oblige. In essence this meant staff would have to be trained quickly (or as was the case self train themselves) ready for the barrage of tight weekly and monthly deadlines.

I tended not to work beyond 6.30/7pm, partly because I was competent at what I did but primarily because I didn't believe in being overworked, exploited for little or no reward, and conforming to an overtime culture. But from what I remember the majority of employees in the companies I worked were more than happy to play the game and work stupid hours. These are hours that can't be given back, but the decision on overtime needs to be made at an individual level and whether it is beneficial or not either monetarily, family or career wise.

In a financial reporting role I had internal and external stakeholders put enormous pressure on me and colleagues to get reports filed on time. A culture of do whatever it takes to please clients and stakeholders existed with idle threats internally of weekend unpaid work if reports were not filed on time coming from senior management. My motto has always been simple; time is money and never work for free.

I firmly believe that we all work to the best of our abilities, of course there are a few exceptions but on the whole we do our best to be professional and adhere to deadlines and company policies. If deadlines are unrealistic and can't be met it is not right to put undue pressure on one individual to get tasks completed on time, without adequate help, remuneration and assistance from colleagues and management. We all can only work in a pressure canister for a certain period of time before something bursts.

It's a dangerous game companies' play by adhering to all client deadlines and requests at any cost. Yes the client pays the bills at the end of day but this doesn't give them the right to dictate fully on their terms. A professional and competent service is required, no question about that, but companies need to be aware that ridiculous and unfair time deadlines will only result in a bad culture, high turnover and a toxic working environment.

Nowadays graduates will be thrown in at the deep end when they start employment. Whilst some might be lucky to avail of on the job or other training the majority will get little or nothing at all and will be expected to learn at a superfast pace. I have no qualms about saying that if I wasn't experienced before I started some of my previous roles I would have found it extremely difficult to stay. Some were high octane, where a fast paced and sink or swim culture existed from the beginning. In one particular role no training was given at all and I had to use my experiences and knowledge to get by in the first few months. When I had time to breathe and come up for the air three months had passed. If I was a graduate coming straight from a degree, I probably would not have survived too long in the company. The reasons being that it would have been too much information to absorb in a short period of time and I wouldn't have had any experience of how to cope in a non training and rapid paced working environment.

So for graduates starting work these days beware and come fully prepared for the organised chaos of many institutions. For experienced professionals the question is do we ever really adapt and adjust to no training, organised chaos, Usain Bolt speed working, and endless deadlines? Well who knows, I certainly find it difficult, but I've managed to adapt so far to everything that has been thrown at me. The sad reality is if we don't adapt we will get left behind.

10. How important is picking the right job

When you finish your college degree, masters or simply your secondary education choosing a job suitable to your needs, personality, wants and career prospects is highly important. The problem that individuals face now is that companies want candidates with experience and are sometimes unwilling to hire on the basis of having degrees and even masters qualifications. In my opinion this is the wrong approach for companies to take, as most qualified students have an enormous amount to offer to companies. So without doubt choosing your first job is important but in the times we live in with very tight employment markets and low salaries, any job might have to do in the short term. If you want to work in the business field as an accountant, economist or stock broker for example you will need the relevant qualifications. Especially in Ireland and the United Kingdom professional qualifications can be looked on more favourably than academic qualifications. Whilst I don't agree with this stance, it appears this is the reality in the current jobs market. Another point to note is that if you spend a certain amount of time in a particular industry, say over five years and decide this field isn't for you, then it will be extremely difficult bordering on impossible to move to another field of work.

The reasons for this are that most companies if not all in Ireland don't view transferable skills as important. They solely look at what work you have been doing in the last few years and make the assumptions on that basis and judge you accordingly. This means that although a candidate might have vast amounts of experience in one field like pensions, accounting, information technology and so on, this experience might be deemed worthless if they want to move to a field like project management.

But if employers were to look deeper at the history and skill sets of potential employees they may find that they are a perfect fit for their company. The secret here is to make sure when you start out in your career that you choose a field of work that you think you may like. It is never too late to change careers and this can be done at any time but it will take a huge sacrifice. You may have to reduce your salary in the short-term and re-educate yourself via a post graduate or masters qualification. In the end the result will justify the means but you will have to be prepared for hardship along the way. If your new career doesn't pay enough it might work as a source of supplementary income. Lecturing, consultancy work and advice to clients are examples here. So for you to change career a huge amount of dedication and commitment to another type of career is needed. You will need to be confident in your abilities and be persistent until you have found your new line of work.

11. A world of endless meetings

A culture of meetings has become the norm in a lot companies especially for employees at medium and senior levels of management. These meetings can last up to two-three hours a day and this has the effect of wasting nearly half the working week in meetings. This filters down to other employees who end up doing the work of the managers who were having the meetings. Meetings can be organised by managers for genuine reasons but more often now they are organised as a sign of power and for something to pass the day by with.

In a company I used work for the head of finance had an idea to have morning shouts daily in every team in the department. What this meant was that for five to ten minutes every morning a member of a team would get up and stand in front of the other team members. He would then go through the workload for the day. Bottlenecks, IT issues, time stealers (as the head of finance used like to say) and so on were discussed. My team was the last to embrace this concept but I did watch the other teams take part in it every morning. On the face of it seemed a good idea. But in reality was it only wasting time or was it something that the head of finance could add to his CV? In busy working environments it is necessary to have catch ups and regular team meetings but weekly should be enough.

Employees need to be trusted that they can do their job, what a morning shout might do is scrutinise everyone's work and possibly have a negative effect. Employees can begin to feel their every move is being watched and this can potentially heighten levels of stress and anxiety. Levels of production decline when one gets the feeling he or she is being watched or someone is standing over their shoulder. If members of staff have spare capacity or downtime they might feel there is a need to mention this promptly to management, or else serious repercussions could be around the corner. Endless meetings can result in a paranoia building up amongst staff that they are constantly being talked about and possibly their jobs are under threat.

This may be extreme, but with a culture of meetings for the sake of meetings a reality in many companies, more thought needs to be given on what effect this can have on staff on the ground. Even communicating minutes of meetings tend to be weak if non-existent, with bland and non descriptive e-mails being sent to team members. Over usage of meetings is an abuse of power but one that is frequently used, and unfortunately not going to stop in the short term.

12. The checklist mentality

Pre the credit crunch and global economic recession of 2007 the majority of large financial institutions took advantage of loose regulation and compliance controls. They traded the markets recklessly and this ultimately led to high scale business failures such as Lehman Brothers in the USA, Northern Rock in the UK, Anglo Irish Bank, AIB and numerous other financial institutions in Ireland. Other mega banks and insurance houses such as AIG had to be bailed out by their respective governments.

Every action has a reaction and unfortunately it took catastrophic financial collapses in numerous countries for governments to act and impose strict and draconian compliance protocols compared to what was perceived as light touch regulation of days gone by. Whilst I will agree that companies are still adapting to these new controls, there is no doubt that enhanced regulation (and possibly over regulation) has brought around a checklist mentality in modern day companies. By checklist mentality I mean the overuse and dependence on checklists to sign off and control work procedures and processes.

For the average worker this has meant more time being spent on filling in needless forms in order to satisfy management that every protocol is being followed correctly. I have noticed in companies recently the increased usage of checklists to the point where internal auditors have asked for certain checklists to be discarded completely or merged with existing ones. In one role I worked in, when I took a step back and counted the amount of checklists I was filling in it bordered on the ludicrous. To get certain reports signed and issued I had to fill in over ten checklists. When I mentioned it to my senior manager I was simply told this is the way it is.

On a personal level I find checklists a hindrance and I know there is the tendency for employees to let the checklist do the thinking and rely on them too heavily. By this I mean when filling them out we tend to be in auto-pilot and tick yes and no, but at the same time not really understanding what we are doing. This is a common problem and one that is overlooked.

For senior management checklists form a de-stress mechanism and are there to prevent anxiety. They prevent active communication as the checklist in theory answers all the questions. If the checklist is signed, all work must be complete and correct, this is the belief anyhow. Whilst at one level I can understand the need for checklists but an over reliance on them can lead to errors. But in a world of compliance and constant need to monitor error and omissions it looks like the checklist mentality of modern day businesses are here to stay.

13. Change management

Whilst studying for my Masters in 2012 I read a very interesting article on change management by Christopher Grey dating back to

2003. By his own admission the piece was polemical in nature but it did get me thinking as to the fascination and over indulgence of companies to be constantly changing their processes and ways of thinking. Grey's argument was in simple terms based around the fact that the majority of companies today tend to want to keep changing and evolving in order to beat the competition and stay one step ahead. A need to be constantly adapting is predominantly discussed. The piece is highly subjective and opinionated but it does resonate with me to the point where I thought does anything in life really change that fast? And if we think the answer is no then why do companies strive for constant change and improvements.

The reality is that change is very slow in business. Many small projects I have worked on have had timescales of six months to one year. The lack of ideas and foresight, as well as poor budget control and resources meant many projects run indefinitely. For the young graduate excited by an ever changing working environment, well I say don't get too excited as you will end up being very disappointed. The recession has meant cutbacks in large scale internal and external projects and in extreme cases an excuse to scrap projects entirely. For some it has became a viable excuse for delays. In fact during a recent study I conducted on delays (for the link to this published study please see my LinkedIn profile) I found apathy sets in for most employees after two years. That is they don't seem to care whether a system or process is implemented if the delay in implementation has taken longer than two years. Before two years the level of interest is heightened, with employees showing a genuine willingness for the system or project to succeed.

One analogy that I thought of and think sums up change management quite well is the following; television was invented in the year 1926 and it was invented as a way to experience moving visual images. The 1950s and 60s saw increased usage by way of box sets in peoples living rooms. The 1970s brought the fight between Betamax and VHS with VHS winning the battle. The 1990s and 2000s brought DVDs, digital and slimmer televisions, HD screens, enhanced colour and sound. But fundamentally from its conception in the 1920s up until today we all by and large watch TV in the same way - in our living rooms. New technologies like iPhone and iPads mean watching TV is more flexible and portable than it has ever been, but the fundamentals are all still the same. I ask you what really has changed. The same analogy can be applied to the office, the majority of us all work in the same way we did twenty to thirty years ago, that is sitting at an office desk, the main difference being e-mail has taken over from the telephone as the primary communication tool. Change is slow; don't be fooled into thinking otherwise.

14. Institutionalised staff

What does it mean to be institutionalised, that is the question. Research has shown prison inmates find it extremely difficult to adjust to the outside world after spending only three, four or five years in prison. Can this simple analogy be translated to the business world? Do employees find it difficult to move jobs or even contemplate moving jobs after a certain time period? Can they adjust to work surroundings easily?

This phenomenon can affect any industry, financial services, law, and information technology and so on. Companies will have rules and norms to fit their needs and these norms and rituals will become embedded into employees' day to day routines without them even realising it. Time alone will not just institutionalise employees. Other factors such as local norms, objectification, personal views and habits will all entrust institutionalisation upon us. Some of us are immune, but most succumb to its advances and dangers.

It can be subjective by nature; some individuals can work in an organisation for two or three years and become institutionalised, for others it will take longer. But the key here is the longer you work for one organisation the more prone you are to become engrained in the belief system and culture and inevitably become *"institutionalised"*. This in itself is not a bad thing. It can promote stability amongst staff. It could be said you are showing loyalty to the hand that feeds you. But on the other hand it can be dangerous to an organisation when blind faith is shown to leadership when glaringly obvious unethical and immoral decisions are taken at board level that can have disastrous consequences for staff and external stakeholders.

A prime example of this happened recently in Ireland in the financial services sector. The leadership of Anglo Irish Bank, AIB, Irish Nationwide, EBS and to a lesser extent Bank of Ireland all made catastrophic decisions regarding their investment portfolio which contributed to Ireland becoming essentially bankrupt. Anglos web of deceit went further as has been succinctly outlined in the national and world press. The senior executives made self absorbed and immoral decisions by allegedly concealing loans and manipulating accounts giving the impression that the bank was in a healthy position when the truth was far from this.

The assigned auditors should have scrutinised and questioned the financial irregularities more closely and their audit of the books can only be described as shoddy at best. They may qualify this by stating the executives' concerned concealed vital financial evidence from them but I ask is it not the auditors remit to discover these irregularities themselves? Other Irish banks behaved appallingly with little or no consideration for the effect it would have on citizens for years to come.

The question is though did anyone at board level or below not suspect something horribly devious was occurring or were they so institutionalised that they thought every move the senior board members made were right. Were they just plain scared to question authority, akin to the unerring respect citizens gave the catholic church for years in Ireland (and globally) until the sickening child abuse scandals broke in the mid 1990s. These are questions that remain unanswered but what we know is the culture that existed in these organisations was toxic and in my opinion institutionalisation of staff helped hide the illusion that the banks were operating in an efficient and healthy manner.

The whole institutionalisation of staff debate can be taken as a given in the public sector. This I will admit is a polemical statement but when staff decide to join the local county councils, police force, become a nurse or prison officer they are invariably signing up for life. Thus it's hard to deny that the comradery and trade union type work arrangements bring about an institutionalisation of staff. Public sector workers tend to be united in their causes, whether striking for better pay or demanding improved working conditions. On the whole they show greater allegiance to the cause and their bond tends to be more solid than in the private sector where if times get tough employees have the advantage of moving on to pastures new. So on this basis it can be deemed that institutionalisation can be good, it can unite staff and form groups that will endeavour to stop exploitation and alienation of workers.

The sad fact is there is no escaping institutionalisation. It will happen to all of us if we stay long enough in the one job. But we need to fight it, as we should always question our companies and managers objectives. We should never get too comfortable in our little bubbles of working styles and should always try to embrace new and changing work practices and technologies. Whilst we should always respect authority to a certain point we should never let it blind us from what is really happening. If a company has become archaic and too old school, it needs fresh ideas and faces to lift it to the next level, and having institutionalised staff can potentially hinder this revival.

I have never worked in a company for longer than three years. Circumstances have dictated where I have ended up working for the large part but there is an underlying tendency I will admit not to getting stuck in the one job or company for too long. Possibly I fear becoming institutionalised. It is an irrational fear akin to being afraid of spiders or flying but in my head it exists. As I have become more experienced in work this train of thought has slowly subsided. Maturity has made this fear virtually redundant in my mind and throwing myself deep into a job for many years is inevitable, it happens to us all.

My fear came from seeing staff in some financial institutions that I have worked for, having an unbreakable faith to the existing corporate culture, even when it has been proven to be at best mildly toxic. Staff with over twenty years service want to leave but at the same time they know they can't, they fear change, a new start, and in their mind have the comfort of nice pensions to look forward to, when in reality these pensions might not be there when they retire (this will be discussed further in chapter four). This head in the sand approach may cost them dear in the future.

In another job I worked in a colleague said to me I need to get out of this job by the time I'm 40. He was 36 at the time and had nearly nine years service completed. Indirectly he was saying to me that he'll be there until he's 40 and even though he denied it, he was now institutionalised. I'm not saying in his case it was a bad thing as he probably liked his job even if it was a very stressful position. But institutionalisation had crept up on him without him realising it. The simple fact here is we can't escape becoming institutionalised, it's part of human nature, it makes work easier, helps get us through the daily grind, creates stability and most importantly de-stresses us and relieves anxiety.

15. Performance reviews

In recent years as the global economy was busy trying to recover the value of performance reviews in companies began to diminish. When I think of performance reviews I always ask *"what benefit do they give"*, or are they *"just a means to an end"*. Companies will justify them by portraying that they are fully committed to the development of employees and they want them to achieve their goals. However these goals tend to be set in stone and are company goals, rarely goals based on the individuals' needs and wants. To make the reviews more valuable and worth doing companies have now linked bonuses to your reviews. Simply put, get a bad review, and get little or no bonus. This may seem unfair, and it probably is, as it can give vindictive managers an excuse to give a bad review to an employee who is performing adequately just on basis of personality traits (whether a manager gets on with a subordinate).

But surely it is time for review processes to become a more collaborative process instead of a one sided dictate on the good and bad of employees. We all need reviews or to be told what we need to improve on or be trained up on, this is a given. But criticisms and reviews need to be constructive and genuine in nature. Ask yourself this, when is the last time you sat through a performance review and thought that was worthwhile? I for one can't remember one instance and I've had a few in my career. They have tended to be tick the box exercises, with human resource departments setting the ball rolling early each year in what they would term the review process. I have on countless occasions been asked to upload goals and objectives to intranets to show that I have something to work towards, but these goals have normally been given to me. I have never once been asked, what are your goals? Instead the process would be *"a do as your told"* exercise. You know what is expected of you, so no excuses now. Will a performance review process like this motivate employees, I doubt it.

In a previous role I worked reviews were carried out every year which was standard practice. Unfortunately the individual carrying out these reviews out lacked the necessary soft skills in communication. His general appreciation of what employees were doing was poor and he was oblivious to how busy they were. His reviews were generic and his motivational tool was to criticise employees and say they needed to improve their attitudes and work outlay. Phrases like, *"you need to get yourself more known on the work floor"* and *"I need to know you're on top of things"* were constantly uttered. Yet not once did he realise how productive the staff were. Not surprisingly this style of review left employees frustrated, angry and unmotivated. Reviewers need to be careful not to over step the mark on criticism. They need to appreciate what employees do and the dedication they show to the cause. Without this, reviewers command no respect and undermine their position.

It's now time for a critical analysis on why companies carry out reviews and what the true worth of them is. Simply uploading goals and having a one to one sit down with a manager is an archaic way of doing it. Collaboration will breed motivation; a more inclusive process will give employees more self worth. Dictating goals and objectives to employees is doomed to failure and will mean performance reviews will be a futile and costly process. We can't take valuable employees for granted; changing work practices mean reviews need to change in tandem.

16. The value of human resource departments in modern business

The value of human resource departments in companies is widely discussed nowadays and there doesn't seem to be a general consensus as to what is the real function and purpose of this area of business. I asked a few colleagues and friends to give their thoughts on HR departments and the responses were mixed. Some saw them as preserving the status quo, as in keeping employees in check, sorting out internal disputes and doing general administrative type tasks. Others saw them as being at the forefront of maintaining a company's external reputation and to clamp down on internal revolt. Others then simply saw the HR employee as a payroll assistant or someone who was there to record sick days and perform performance reviews once or twice a year. None of these three assumptions came from individuals who work in the area of HR.

All these assumptions of what HR do and don't do are not far wide of the mark. The key question here is do modern day companies really need and can they afford HR departments. HR managers and heads of departments can earn attractive salaries for little or no perceived return to the company. My thinking here is that I have seen no indication or reason to see HR departments as something other than mind numbing and interfering departments as far as the normal operational employee is concerned. The only time I have ever come in contact with HR employees is when they have been part of the interviewing process, a performance review process and unfortunately a redundancy programme. During interview processes HR employees will tend to observe and take notes, to see how the candidate performs and reacts to difficult and taxing questions. They will also have a list of maybe five to six questions of their own to see how you respond or have responded in certain work situations. But in reality the manager of the department you are interviewing for will ultimately make the decision on whether you get the job or not. HR will simply tie up the loose ends, be it salary negotiation and reference checking. The same process tends to happen in performance reviews were a HR employee will observe and tick boxes to see if the person being reviewed is adhering to company policies of performance. As for redundancy, normally they'll give you a cheque and send you on your merry way with little or no thanks for your commitment to the company.

My argument is polemical by nature but deliberately so. We need to start thinking outside the box on the value of HR departments. Being able to mediate in internal disputes, perform various administration tasks, perform reviews and have the so called soft skills should not be enough to justify their professional existence. Having soft skills or being perceived to have is not a money generating skill. Soft skills are of vital importance but to managers and individuals leading the business, not to administration driven roles.

The majority of jobs nowadays are time driven and cost critical. How does HR comply with this? How to fix the perceived negative views of HR departments in the marketplace is tricky and will take time. Their roles need to be broadened and employees need to feel that they are there to protect them, not just the company name and reputation. Recent moves on HR departments to align themselves with strategic decision makers in companies might be an interesting idea. But surely the modern day HR department has to go back to basics and reinvent themselves from an administration driven environment that to all self and purposes seems outdated and worthless. Remember time is money and HR is a cost gone too far. It needs to be radically reinvented in order to survive.

On the positive side there is an area that HR employees can exploit and this is the ever growing area of project management. Project management has become a buzz term recently but there is no denying its importance, and at the heart of it is a necessity for people management. Here is where the skilled and experienced HR employee can come into play. Managing people in stressful project based environments will help companies to ultimately achieve their project aims. It's in an area like this that HR can improve a company's profitability by reducing delays and keeping projects on track. By getting involved in areas like this HR employees will begin to fulfil their professional needs better.

17. Recruitment agencies – A true skill?

Recruitment agencies will undoubtedly pontificate about the value of their chosen art, but for my reckoning it's a skill that we as potential employees can on most occasions do without. I'm sure some of you reading this, will query my line of thinking and this is probably because recruitment agencies have been good to you. There is no denying that when a competent and proactive recruiter listens to the client, then and only then will this process bear fruit for the client. But a lack of basic listening and communication skills is a glaring problem that riddles the recruitment agency industry.

In my professional career so far, I have worked for numerous organisations and only twice have I landed positions through a recruitment agency. I found my first experience off-putting to say the least. I had just arrived back from a sabbatical in Australia and wanted to get back into the workforce primarily because I was broke but I wanted to start rebuilding my career again. After using online websites and adverts for jobs before, I decided going the recruitment agency route would be best on this occasion. I met a few agencies and all were impressed with my CV and said we should aim for the best salary possible. I thought that sounds promising but there was little talk about what actual role would suit me.

As I had worked as an accountant for the previous five years it was assumed (and it will always be assumed) that I wanted another job as an accountant. On this occasion I wasn't overly bothered what role I landed as I needed to be back earning again.

However if you want to change careers or sidestep in an industry then recruitment agencies will invariably not be too interested in you unless they think you can land and command a large salary. Remember recruitment agencies are only interested in commission and increasing their profits. Don't be fooled here, recruitment agencies are businesses. My experience was one where I was constantly harassed and virtually forced to take a role I was offered as the recruiter stated that it was the salary they had promised. Yes it was the salary they had promised but it wasn't them paying it or who had just sat through two gruelling interviews to get the offer in the first place.

Recruiters will normally strike just after you have finished the interview (some even ring during the interview). They know you're tired and will more than likely agree to what they are saying just to get them off the phone. They will ask you how you thought you did and if you think this was a role that you would like. Really what they are saying is "*I would love if you got offered and accepted this role as I will make some commission*". Commission, mmm!

I ended up accepting a role I didn't like and only spent six months in it. Now the decision to take the job and only spent six months there was my doing, but I wonder if I wasn't harassed and dictated to on the values of this company and job, if I would have accepted it in the first place. The answer is I will never really know, but my educated guess is I would have said no. Ever since that unpleasant experience I have always threaded carefully with recruitment agencies. A recent positive experience with a recruiter has changed my mind slightly but predominantly my experiences have been negative.

There is a major issue that traditional recruiters now have to face up to and that is social media sites like LinkedIn stealing a march on them. LinkedIn have been very clever in their approach, slowly building a wide base of users over the last few years. Now companies can advertise positions on this website. Individuals can in effect post an online CV that shows off their skill set and capabilities. Facebook search as well as proven to be a growing market for companies to recruit on. The question now is how will recruiters respond to this threat? Some online recruiters like webrecruit.ie offer a traditional recruitment service but at substantially lower prices, with fees based on client salaries. The world of recruitment agencies is changing, the big guns won't have it all their own way anymore, its time they adapted or face ruin. An increasingly competitive recruitment market has forced recruiters to expand their range of services. Market research services, writing white papers on various topics and communication services are now marketed. Below are some advantages and disadvantages of traditional recruiters, see what you think;

Advantages
- Some companies prefer to outsource hiring to recruiters as they view it internally as time consuming, a waste of resources and ultimately cost ineffective
- Recruiters can go through potential candidates and eliminate what they perceive to be *"poor fits"*

- Can be good for executive type roles where an individual prefers to use an *"agent"* to do the searching for her
- Can take the pain away from searching endless websites for jobs if you know exactly what you want (this is seldom the case)
- They may have a good relationship with particular clients who only use recruitment agencies
- Like football agents they can and should negotiate a better deal for the client regarding salary and benefits
- As they are primarily fee and commission based they will chase up clients to see if interviews will happen or to see how interviews have gone.
- They do all the organising regarding interviews, but remember this is the easy part and getting a job is 99.99% down to the candidate
- They can on occasion derive feedback from clients on why candidates were unsuccessful at interview but again from my experience organisations tend to give back generic feedback which on balance is of no use to anyone.
- Most if not all employers use software packages to scan CVs for the perfect match when candidates send in their CVs via advertisements on job boards. Agencies can send CVs in direct and cut straight through this process.

Disadvantages

- Can be quick to dismiss adequate candidates because of what they perceive as inadequacies
- Not good for anyone trying to change career path or even trying to do something different within an industry i.e. moving from web design to programming, financial reporting to fund accounting
- They will harass clients into taking the best paying roles even when not suitable
- Not interested in helping clients who appear to be interested in multiple roles
- Poor communicators and listeners
- Will invariably always assume if you work in one field, than that's the area you would like to stay in
- Never read CVs properly and can on occasion but you forward for jobs in companies you have worked in already (it's happened to me)
- Can put you forward for jobs without informing you (it's happened to me)
- For companies using them the fees they charge can be outrageous, sometime 25-30% of the salary of a potential candidate
- They tend to scan search engines and social media sites to increase their client base

- Are always sending you on information on jobs that you would never have any interest working on
- Pretend to be your friends with cold calls checking if you are happy in your current role
- Will ring you up talking about a job they have on their books when they don't even have a job specification and when the likelihood is that they have no relationship with the hiring organisation
- When quizzed on details about hiring company policies will invariably come up with some nonsense to sidestep the question. Example being when I asked once if there was a canteen in a company I agreed to join, the agency stated there was because it was a large company. I also asked did this particular company pay overtime and to confirm the working hours. When I started working there I found there was no canteen, they didn't pay overtime, the working day was 9 – 5.15, not 9-5.30 and the working culture was overtime driven
- Don't be fooled, they are just out for themselves, they have absolutely no genuine interest in you, only the fact that they see $ signs. Commission, Commission, Commission
- They will say every company is a great company to work for with great future prospects – the reality is they don't have a clue regarding this. They are just guessing.
- If you are out of work whether on a career or forced break, some agencies are not accommodating regarding meeting you. An example I experienced - I was out of work looking

after my kids' full time. An agency rang me with an interesting role. I said I would like to be put forward for the role. My flexibility was limited as I was looking after my kids full-time; therefore I asked if an interview could be sorted for a Monday at any time. Eventually after a lot of hassle with the agency saying the company would not interview on Monday, when they did actually ask the company they agreed to it. The first part had been organised and I was all set and preparing for the interview. The agency then got back to me stating I couldn't attend the interview unless I went in and met with them physically to discuss what might come up. I said this would be difficult for me but I would make time on a Wednesday evening before the interview the following Monday and come in. I said I would be in for 5.15/5.30pm as my wife would leave work early. The agency stated they finished at 5pm and were unwilling to stay later for the proposed meeting. I stated again I had two kids to look after and I was making sacrifices at my end to come in. I appreciate I needed a job and fundamentally it is up to me to make sacrifices but the realities of life sometimes make this difficult and compromise is needed. When the agency was adamant they couldn't meet on the Wednesday evening I proposed a Skype call or phone interview. Again both were declined. With such technologies available as Skype there was no excuse for the agency to decline this invitation. Eventually the agency withdrew my application and I couldn't attend the interview. Suffice to say I will never use this particular agency again or recommend their services. Their lack of professionalism and flexibility was appalling. It disgusted me. It is this way of dealing with candidates that give recruitment agencies a bad name.

18. Poor communication

There is no understating the importance of communication in the workplace, but unfortunately it is something we don't seem to be improving upon. It's a subject that has been written on extensively so it's not something I wish to write about in depth. In fact communication is now so important to modern business that most large multinationals and those especially in the public eye tend to have a dedicated team look after communications. Ryanair are synonymous for using their head of communications to liaise with the media when instances of embarrassment come to light. Admitting they were thinking of charging passengers to use the toilets on board their aircrafts was ludicrous. But good communication departments can put a good spin on events to make them an advertising dream. Communication issues have certainly never stopped Ryanair in dominating its chosen field.

With more women entering the jobs market in Ireland since the mid 1990s communication was forecasted to improve. If anything what we have learnt is that the advent of a more mixed working environment has brought more difficulty in this area. Modern technologies (especially e-mail, smart-phone, texting) may be butchering the English language but whatever reasons we come up with we seem no closer to solving the communication conundrum. Women have better soft skills; Men are poor communicators, is this true? These are two myths that get banded about in the management speak of today. Ryanair's last two communication heads have been male. Is there a particular reason for this? Who knows? Do they think men are better communicators or where they the only viable candidates. My own experience would conclude that both men and women have many faults when it comes to good communication in the workplace.

I have found that some men have better soft skills but are not necessarily good at engaging them. They can be more introverted and in some instances condescending. My experience of women colleagues has been that their communication methods are more direct and forceful and they can exert power in a more controlling and psychological way. These are just my thoughts and experiences, to get you thinking. As humans we are not great at admitting fault and can pass the blame on to others. This can be very easy to do when someone is in a position of authority and it is something I have experienced myself. Authority figures will never admit they are wrong as that is conceding they have faults in their working style.

In theory the best communication should happen with a mix of both sexes working in tandem, but this is too simplistic a solution. There is no easy fix and whatever job we do or work situation we encounter communication and most likely poor communication will be at the heart of it. It's the people we work with that form a large basis for why we stay in particular jobs and companies. Therefore communication amongst colleagues has to be prioritised.

19. Work life balance

As the Dolly Parton song goes the traditional working day is nine to five, but depending on what you do and where you are from this nine to five can be anything from 6am to 12 midnight. Working culture can play a part in how you work, Americans are perceived as having a *"live to work"* culture with their long working days and low annual leave entitlements. European counterparts are perceived as being a more *"work to live"* culture but this doesn't mean they work any less diligently or harder than anyone else. Perception can be misleading when it comes to work.

But regardless of perception, a company's working culture, policies and ethics will dictate the hours and severity of your work. This will then translate into a good work life balance or as in some companies a poor one. Yes we don't have to work every hour God sends but sometimes we as human beings feel obliged to bow to every wish of our employers. Whilst I am not an advocate of working overtime (and certainly when you don't get paid for it), I do understand the pressures put on employees especially in times of economic difficulty and work insecurity.

All of this adds up to a poor work life balance. Work long hours continuously and eventually the body and mind will begin to shut down in the form of burnout, increased anxiety, stress and poor health. We don't have to work overtime. A company should be structured so that it includes a work life balance where normal working hours are adhered to. Unfortunately I'm a realist and I have worked in too many companies to realise that reality and expectation are two different things altogether. We will all end up working overtime, such is life. Employers abiding by a proper work life balance system should include the following or some of them in their working policies.

Flexi-time - this means hours can be built up on an electronic clock card which can be used to take days off. The rules of flexitime differ in the companies that operate it (which are few and predominately in public sector companies) but essentially it is a reward for extra time worked and built up. It can include a flexible starting or leaving time but core hours where one has to be in work are normally 10am to 4pm with a minimum of seven hours being worked in one day or 35 hours worked each week. I have enjoyed the luxury of flexitime in some of the companies I have worked in and it doesn't diminish the quality of work completed. It is a great perk to have especially if you have kids and it is hard to put a monetary value on it. If employees abuse the system it is simply taken away.

On-site childcare or crèche facilities – yes this may be asking too much but there are companies who have on-site crèche facilities. If this is impractical as I'm sure it is for many companies a childcare subsidy would help the burden put on parents by exorbitant costs associated with raring children. Some companies do offer subsidies but they tend to be low at circa 10% and tend to be limited to the larger branded childcare facilities.

No overtime – keeping overtime to a minimum or not having it in the first place is a good way of promoting a vibrant work life balance by an employer. Overtime can be dictated by managers, poor work structures, poor delegation, unrealistic and unreasonable deadlines, but in my own opinion a well oiled and well run company should be eradicating overtime or not entertaining it all. If overtime needs to be done (reporting year end deadlines etc) it should be relayed to employees as early as possible and crucially compensation should be of a high level for the work done.

Be adequately staffed and not overworking employees – this point leads on from the no overtime one above. If a work life balance is to be achieved it is not acceptable to over work employees, whether this is caused by not being adequately staffed, poor management, poor delegation or sheer laziness on the part of other colleagues. No employee should tolerate deliberate over delegation of tasks to them and if this is the case management should be informed. If the company promotes an unrealistic workload for employees then for the sake of one's health and family life, alternative measures like searching for a new job might be the best option

Home or remote access work – depending on your job and the sensitivity of the information you work with remote access work should be available to you. However some companies use it and others don't. For employees who have a long commute or have kids that need to dropped to crèche or school, working from home can provide some relief from the daily grind of tiresome and exhausting travel. Yahoo in the past few years pulled back on offering work from home arrangements citing that productivity was suffering. Whilst there is no real proof of a reduction in productivity due to working from home, some companies prefer to have employees in the office all the time as it is easier to communicate and face to face contact is deemed more beneficial. Whatever the view of the company you work for there is no doubting that remote access or home work is a good policy to employ as part of a work life balance program.

Extra holidays for new parents – maternity leave and in some countries paternity leave is compulsory and available to be taken. Some companies give paternity leave but in Ireland this is limited. Obviously extra leave is at the discretion of the employer but any leave given always looks favourable and can do no harm reputational wise. It can be seen by employees as a nice reward for hard work and recognition of how difficult the first few weeks of parenthood can be. From my own experience some companies do give parental leave and normally this ranges from two to five working days. But some don't and this can be an extra hardship on already suffering parents.

If a company wants to promote a good work life balance then extra parental leave is a nice way to achieve this. Even at a basic level, support and understanding for parents when their children are sick would be nice as many childcare facilities will not allow sick children attend their facility. This can mean busy parents taking time off as they simply have no choice but to look after their children. Whilst from an employer's perspective this situation is not ideal it is unfortunately a necessity for parents.

Proper training of staff – adequate training is essential to relieve anxiety and the difficulty that comes with starting a new job or changing a functional part of your job. We have all been in a situation where on the job or external training has been lacking when needed most. This can enhance your stress levels and this stress can be taken home with you, effecting your home and family life. While this scenario may seem extreme, it is true. It has happened to me in previous roles where training was non-existent and this left me in a position where I was stressing on whether I could get a particular process completed on time and correctly. I used take this stress home with me. As Roy Keane (ex footballer and current assistant manager of the Ireland football team) stated, *"Fail to prepare, prepare to fail"*. Training is an essential part of any work life balance program, as employees need to feel comfortable in their jobs.

Subsidised canteens and study support – the surprising thing here is that a lot of companies don't have canteens in the first place. Once subsidised, they can ease the financial burden of eating out at lunchtime. On the other hand they can prove too convenient for employees and also a way to grab a quick sandwich so that the day's workflow isn't disturbed. This might be seen by some employees as a way of keeping them in-house and limiting visiting other shops and restaurants on the outside. Depending on your viewpoint they can work either way but for me they are essential. Educational support was one of the first areas to suffer cutbacks during the recession, but to promote staff retention monetary assistance for tuition is essential.

20. Business ethics – Do they exist?

We all endeavour to be as ethical as possible, but in a capitalist society where money and profits are the key drivers and determinants of success our ideologies and values can get left to one side. This overwhelming fascination with money and finance can lead to a society that is corrupt, greedy and in the business world an unethical corporate culture.

It would be unfair and wrong to tarnish every person or company with the same brush, as this is just not the case. Employees make a choice to be ethical but their beliefs can get distorted by the company hierarchy they work for. They may enter their company with an open mind but after many years of service, they can become institutionalised and engrained in a corporate culture that is toxic. Their judgement can get blinded by extra money, perks, junkets, and the so called high life. Greed can take over and what were once our core beliefs become a distant memory. Yes it may seem extreme that us humans get easily led and dictated to by the power of money but sadly recent history show prime examples of this behaviour.

As mentioned earlier in the chapter, FIFA the world's football governing body has been beset by constant allegations of corruption and unethical behaviour. The world cup bids that were eventually won by Russia for 2018 and Qatar for 2022 have been tainted by accusations of bribes and vote rigging. Whilst these accusations have not been proven the belief amongst the general public is that they are true. Because of FIFAs stance of self investigation and tarnished reputation the average football supporter and spectator can only suspect that corruption and unethical policies are rife in FIFA. The arrogance of their President Sepp Blatter does not help but if an organisation is allowed to be run like an old school dictatorship then unethical behaviour will cultivate amongst all levels.

The recent world banking crisis left many individuals jobless and companies bankrupt. The root cause will always be speculated to be the bad and unethical polices that were at practice in numerous worldwide organisations, from Lehman Brothers in America, Northern Rock in the UK, Anglo Irish Bank in Ireland and so on. The list is unfortunately endless. Some governments didn't cover themselves in glory as well. But just when you think these

69

companies have learnt their lessons of past mistakes, a culture of unethical bonuses and payments is now also becoming apparent in some organisations.

AIG received the largest government bailout of a private company in U.S. history. This became necessary after the insurance company was technically bankrupt. Without this facility thousands of jobs would have been lost and the impact on the financial markets catastrophic. The US government didn't want another large institution to go under after what had happened to Lehman Brothers.

It is fair to say and somewhat of an understatement that serious mistakes were made by the AIG board in the lead up to the world financial crisis. This however did not prevent it announcing on March 17, 2009 that they were paying $165 million in executive bonuses, according to U.S. news reports. President Barack Obama, who voted for the AIG bailout as a Senator stated

"It's hard to understand how derivative traders at AIG warranted any bonuses, much less $165 million in extra pay. How do they justify this outrage to the taxpayers who are keeping the company afloat?"

You would have to agree with the most powerful man in the world when he asserts his anger at the proposed bonuses. Is this just pure ignorance on the part of a company board out of touch with the reality of today's business world or more of the old school unethical and socially unjust corporate behaviour? Have lessons of the past been learnt or is the greed mentality of corporate suits beginning to fester out of control once more. The signs are ominous.

In my own country of Ireland it was reported in late 2014 that Irish Water (a recently set up state body to charge homeowners for the consumption of water) was going to pay bonuses to staff even though the company was now technically been paid by the public and taxpayer. The head of the company John Tierney as of November 2014 failed to acknowledge that these bonuses were unjust and calls for his resignation went on deaf ears. In 2015 when the average family struggle to pay bills and keep financially afloat, unethical and greedy policies of companies such as Irish Water should not be allowed to go on unchallenged. Currently public anger is growing in Ireland with numerous demonstrations held against the water charges and establishment of the company. Whilst I don't agree with the methods being used by the demonstrators' I do fully understand why they are opposed to paying the charges. For most they simply can't afford it. Governments now need to enact laws and provisions to stop unjustified and basically unearned bonuses being allocated to individuals who simply do not deserve them. Whilst this is tricky to do in the private sector (and technically illegal in most cases), it shouldn't prove so difficult in a state owned institution once the will is there to enact such policies preventing payment.

Whilst the above examples are only a few of what exists they do show that business ethics are lacking in many organisations. The optimist in me hopes that these are isolated cases but the reality is somewhat different I fear.

Chapter 2

Management Speak

Introduction

Fans of the British version of the hit television show The Office will remember the arrogant and humourous character David Brent. A manager who didn't take himself too seriously and was hilariously inept at getting his team to bond and gel together to the point he became the butt of office jokes. It was a fantastic show that highlighted how easy it is for egotistical and limited people to get into management yet at the same time thinking they are fantastic at their jobs and that their team and colleagues love them. The programme was a comedy and that's the level it is meant to be taken at but there were hidden meanings to the programme that were not that far from the truth.

David Brent's character once said in an episode *"if you're going to be late, make sure you're an hour late and have a good breakfast"*. I still smile every time I think of the line. It's a gem and wouldn't it be great if all our managers had a sense of humour like this. Unfortunately the majority don't and are workaholics.

Managers and employees alike utter a plethora of irritating and cringe worthy expressions. Some are mildly irritating, some bearable but others will eat away at you every time you hear them. They can become soul destroying, but the sad thing is managers and colleagues who blurt these out actually mean them and some even think they are funny. Here is my list of over forty common phrases heard on the office floor. Some you will have heard before, some will be new but what is for sure is that you will definitely hear these again at some point during your career.

50 phrases heard on the office floor

1. *Are you winning?*

I'm still not fully sure where this expression originated but for my reckoning it has to be the most annoying saying doing the rounds in the modern day office floor. The kind of person who uses this expression thinks they are funny and humorous, yet by using it they are invariably going to annoy the person they are talking with to such a degree that they may try to avoid you at every opportunity.

I've lost count of the amount of times it has been said to be; now I tend to ignore it and let it wash over my head. Managers will use it and it is an indirect way of saying I hope your work is done and there are no unforeseen problems around the corner. It only became popular in the last five years, but the sooner it disappears, the better. I considered calling the book *"are you winning"* but I didn't want to antagonise people any further, mentioning it is enough.

2. *You got to up your game*

This expression to me has a sporting context and has been ripped off, possibly from American football or a physical team sport like rugby union or Irish hurling. It should never be used in an office environment but many managers will use it astonishingly as a supposed motivational tool. They will say in front of you that *"you need to up your game"*, that is you need to start working harder and possibly getting deadlines adhered to quicker.

I first heard it twelve years ago when a geeky manager reprimanded a colleague and uttered this magical phrase. Other colleagues laughed and that is the response it deserves, it's a laughable expression that is only used by poor communicators who don't know how else to get the best out of their employees. It comes a close second to *"are you winning"* for cringe worthiness, but just falls short.

3. *Are you on a half day (When you go home at 5pm)*

When this phrase is heard on the office floor, it can be assumed there is an undercurrent of overtime in the company. It is a sly remark that is normally made by managers who are firing an underhand jibe at a colleague for going home at a reasonable and normal hour. This phrase was commonly used in one financial services company I worked where crazy overtime and weekend work was the norm. This company wasn't a leader when it came to having a work life balance. People who use this expression are not funny, they are pathetic and need to take a good close look at their work ethic and the kind of example they are setting for other members of their team. It's a sad saying, said by sad people. Thankfully it's on the decline but it can still be heard on many an office floor.

4. *Keep me in the loop (Keep me posted)*

This saying is very common globally. It typically means that colleagues should be kept up to speed on current events or important happenings in the company which are relevant to the team or department they are in. The main problem I have with it is in essence it doesn't really mean anything at all. Outside the office floor, I would hardly say to a friend "*to keep me in the loop*" regarding any important matter. It doesn't sound right and is by all accounts a nothing expression. I honestly don't think I have ever used this saying but I'm sure I will sometime. It's like sheep running off a cliff, once one does it, all the sheep do and this saying has a little bit of that in it. "*Keep me posted*" is a lighter form of it but still management speak.

5. *Is it that time already? / Where did the day go?*

By the sounds of it admittedly the above phrase might not sound annoying. The context in which it is heard is important. Think of working a long day in an office and genuinely putting in a good performance. The boss swans around the place, in and out of meetings, making pointless phone calls all to waste time and give the impression he is run off his feet. 5pm comes around and he blurts out "*is it that time already*" or worse "*where did the day go*" Hear it every day for a while and it will drive you spare. From my own experience individuals who are border-line useless and detrimental to the company because of poor and inferior performance use this phrase.

There is nothing worse than being bored to distraction in work as the day can drag. This can be painful, but someone who wallows in this and then has the audacity to intimate that he had been worked off his feet by using the above phrase should be ashamed and duly take a good hard look at the work morals and ethics he adheres to.

6. *Business day one and (T+1)*

For the first five years of my career I was working in the Fund Management industry and monthly deadlines was the norm. Month after month, the phrase *"business day one"* was used to describe working day one of every month. It is now embedded in to the management speak of funds and many deadline driven businesses to the detriment of the English language.

T+1, T+2 and so on are in my opinion an irritating code to describe trade date plus one day, trade date plus two days, etc. It simply means trades or security transactions will settle in the financial markets in one or two days after the trade date. This coded language is now embedded in the culture of companies who trade securities. Managers to appear knowledgeable tend to talk in coded language to describe business functions.

7. *You need to be more proactive?*

My answer to this question is, do you? Proactive is one of those over used words in management speak today. It is used as some misguided form of motivation. I will freely admit that at times I can lack motivation. I am always professional and I have never needed to be proactive to get tasks done efficiently and within any deadlines given. When someone tells me I need to be more proactive, it has the reverse psychological effect on me, I tend to work even slower, a protest of sorts. Whilst I agree being proactive can help in certain circumstances, the underlying way in which this phrase is used has always infuriated me. In real terms very few people are proactive. We all work at our own pace and have our own unique styles of work and we certainly don't need to be told from anyone to be more proactive.

We should be judged on results and competency, not how quick we get something done. Being proactive and making blundering errors is of no help to anyone, well only if we learn from them, but then most companies brush errors under the carpet, as if they don't its admitting something wrong happened in the first place. In simple terms the term *"proactive"* needs to be reined in. A passive worker who sits at his task and performs his tasks admirably is just as good as the active worker who runs around the place and gets his tasks completed. We just have become brainwashed into believing proactive is better. Is it? I've yet to be convinced.

8. *Its critical, crucial, imperative, vital (that deadlines are met)*

In today's hyper busy environment every task is client driven and needs to be completed ridiculously quick, well this is what we are told. Companies compete against each other to poach clients and when these clients are on their books they need to be able to bill for any work completed. This leads to extra stress and workload being cast upon the low level worker who has to perform tasks as if their lives depended on it.

Deadlines can't be missed, even if goals are unrealistic. In this sort of crazy office environment which is all too common, words like critical, vital, crucial and imperative get banded about with ease to the point they become meaningless. Think about how many times a manager has said to you that it is crucial, imperative, vital and most importantly critical that a task get completed on time. You would need a lot of fingers to count them. It happens every day. These words begin to be used out of context and are an easy way for a manager and poor communicators to issue idle threats to co-workers. The thing to realise is that nothing is crucial or imperative; it's all subjective and relative. It can be a case of client power getting out of control. Now every time a manager utters these words I just smile, as I am fully aware of what is critical, vital, imperative and crucial in my professional and private life, I hope you are too.

9. *You got to hit the ground running*

In today's hectic and non training environment in global businesses, being able to show your skill set and proficiency from the start of any job is a necessity. This is a given now, unless you are a graduate straight from college, but even still, graduates need to show a level of competency. This is where the saying "*you got to hit the ground running*" comes in. It is an overly used phrase that tends to be an escape clause for incompetent managers who use it as a means to attack colleagues and subordinates by insinuating that they are not performing their tasks and duties to the required standard.

I firmly believe it should never be used in the first place. New starters have a stressful enough time in any job, then wanting to listen to a manager utter this nonsense of a phrase. I haven't had the pleasure that often of hearing it but I did get told once that it was expected that I hit the ground running in one job. I took it indirectly to mean its sink or swim in this job and we won't be throwing you armbands either.

10. *I need to make sure we are on the same page*

What page is this I ask? We've all been stuck in meetings where we don't have the first clue what the speaker or chairperson is talking about. We pretend we do by nodding our head and keeping eye contact and looking interested. Most human beings attention spans are short, in some cases fifteen, twenty seconds, some might last a minute or two. The fact is we all switch off after a certain period of

81

time. This is when interpretations of meetings and meanings of speeches can get lost in translation.

I might take something different from a meeting then you did and so on. It doesn't mean either of us is necessarily wrong but what it might mean is that we are now not on the "*same page*". Walk around any office floor and you'll hear someone in the background saying either by phone or by asking someone directly if we are on the "*same page*". This phrase is heard every day without fail in office departments.

11. I've been chasing my tail all day

This phrase is common in occurrence. It simply means that we haven't had a minute to ourselves all day. When one task is completed the next hits us immediately and so on. It can be said to justify an individuals' existence on the work floor by making colleagues think that an individual has been working hard all day. We all know people like this. I've mostly heard women using this expression but that is not to say men don't use it as well. The trick is not to be chasing your tail all day, delegate tasks and be competent in what you do. No matter what style we use for work this phrase will never disappear.

12. We operate an open door policy around here

This will tend to be heard when starting a new job. It will be said by managers and directors who want to give the impression of a relaxing and open office. But the undertone to this is quite different in most cases. The open door policy referred to tends to be anything but open. In fact most directors and high flyers don't want to be disturbed by individuals they perceive as lower in the food chain.

Not a particularly funny or annoying phrase just one that is typically said to save face and look good. In a previous job I worked in I had the pleasure of having to get payments in excess of €250,000 signed by directors in the company. It was one thing finding them in their office, (most times you had to interrupt meetings or so called meetings to get their signature) but if you were lucky enough to do it was an ordeal getting a signature. You were looked at with disdain for disturbing their wonderful little world and then they would initial the payment, grunt and indirectly tell you to "*f**k off*". I don't miss those days. That was my experience of "*we operate an open door policy*" Beware of this phrase!

13. This is coming down the pipeline

Yes an all time classic. It refers to new procedures, processes and systems that will be implemented in the future. It can be construed as an indirect way of telling someone to prepare for bedlam and chaos down the line or pipeline as it is now. I always operate a rule of three in business that is if a manager states that a system will be implemented in six months the likelihood is it will take at least eighteen months before it will go live. I can't help myself by using these phrases such as "*go live*". I have been working in an office too long, maybe time for a change down the pipeline.

14. Let's have a catch up

A common phrase heard today but one with a double meaning. Firstly it can mean a chat is needed to discuss something important that has come up. This could mean being gone for five minutes or five hours, it depends on the importance of the issue at hand.

Alternatively it could mean something totally different. A former manager I worked for in a financial services company used to say to me, can we have "*a catch-up*". What this really meant was I am now going to tell you exactly what I think of you and what you should be doing to become an important team player (in her eyes anyhow). Every two months I would receive an invite to a meeting with the title "*catch up*". It was my review of sorts and a chance for my manager whose managerial style wouldn't have looked out of place in a circus to berate me and show me her true colours. Depending on the context, this phrase may not be so friendly and innocent after all.

15. Its BAU (business as usual)

When I first heard BAU being mentioned I didn't have a clue what it meant. I needed to ask my manager at the time to explain it. But it appears this phrase has been bandied around organisations for a long time and simply means a function or process that has become a normal part of the working day. Outside of the business world the phrase is meaningless.

16. Is it a game changer, show stopper or deal breaker?

Well is it? I have always wondered, what really is a game changer, show stopper or deal breaker in a business context? It's hard to tell, because on the face of things, is anything really that important. The *"game changer"* phrase has been taken straight from sport where it is used to describe possible shifts in momentum in games. The *"deal breaker"* phrase is common in most contexts. Again *"show stopper"* means the same as the two other phrases and is possibly used more in the office. In essence all three phrases allude to something that may have potential consequences in the work flow of a process or procedure.

17. Can you park that?

This doesn't mean that you need to go outside and park your car. What it means in a business context is can you stop what you are doing and now concentrate on some other task that has been deemed more important. I have heard this saying in every company I have worked in, it has seamlessly made its way into the professional working domain without much notice. From my perspective it is poor use of the English language and should not be used at all.

18. Did you flag that?

This phrase was a favourite of a colleague I used work for. He used always ask *"did you flag that?"* to the appropriate individual when problems occurred or if potential problems were on the horizon. The phrase is meaningless on its own but in the office environment it simply means, has a certain issue, event, or problem been notified to the correct person in the company, i.e. somebody possibly of a high standing that needs to know what is going on. As with certain other phrases it can be misused, overused and used to pass the blame of one person's forgetfulness on to another. For example a manager may be responsible for letting another colleague know about an error in a financial investment report, but simply to apportion blame and relieve anxiety passes this responsibility onto a subordinate. Now it's this individual's responsibility and he better flag that problem quickly to the boss!

19. That needs to be ironed out

No not the crease out of your favourite shirt but a work problem that has festered out of control and needs to be fixed. By ironing out something it is assumed a problem will be analysed and eventually solved. It is now so engrained in daily management speak that this mildly annoying phrase is unlikely to disappear anytime soon

20. You need to take ownership of this.

This phrase is self explanatory in the sense it means that one must be fully responsible for the tasks they are designated and be trusted to perform these tasks unaided and independently whilst maintaining high levels of quality. This is fair enough, but from my own experience of this phrase it can be a means for managers to get subordinates to perform tasks they should be performing themselves or are incapable of performing and need such incompetence covered up. The phrase is needed in the workplace, as tasks and projects can become delayed if proper delegation and ownership of them is not adhered to.

21. Has that been peer reviewed?

We live in a world of compliance and checklists. Unfortunately for the average worker this means anything they prepare or complete needs to be checked by a superior or colleague. Peer can mean anything in the context of checking but at its simplest level it means that someone else has cast their eyes over a document that was prepared by you. When something important is handed for final sign off or is to be sent externally via email or by post, invariably someone in the office is going to say "*has that been peer reviewed*"?

22. Can you prioritise this?

This phrase is used by managers and employees who want something done rapidly. They don't care what you are currently doing or how important it is. Managers can exert their power by demanding work flow items are prioritised, this is their prerogative and more often than not they will utilise this power. The problem with the over use of this phrase is that every little item or task becomes important. The reality is that not everything is important enough to be prioritised, but try telling that to some superiors or colleagues.

23. Have you not been trained in on this?

The urban myth out there is that modern companies embrace good training programs and value training of employees as essential. My experience has taught me that training in companies is very limited and the training that does exist tends to be self training or a form of on the job training which can be poor. Regardless of training or experience levels, after a few months in most jobs an employee is expected to have grasped their role to the point where little or no guidance is necessary. This is the reality albeit unrealistic to most people.

A common scenario will develop in any job. An employee will be asked to perform a task that they have received no training for and simply can't do. It may be that they should have prior experience to carry out the task but more often than not it is a task unique to a particular job or company. They simply would not know how to do the task through no fault of their own. They sit and ponder for a while and then decide to ask a colleague or manager for help, anxious of the response that will await them. Then the old gem comes out, *"have you not been trained on this"*. The assumption is always there with superiors that their colleagues and team members have been trained on everything, yet most know full well that training has not been forthcoming. My advice for when this phrase is heard, is not to get angry, it is just an unfortunate part of modern day office life.

24. Drill down (when using Microsoft excel)

For experienced workers who are well a customised to using Microsoft excel, the phrase drill-down will not be new. In fact it is all most taken for granted that such a phrase be stated in the midst of use. I for one was confused when someone said to me first to drill down on a spreadsheet. I looked perplexed at my colleague until the penny dropped and I finally understood what he meant. All he was asking was to move or scroll down on a particular spreadsheet to find a number or cell. The phrase can have different meanings depending on the context of use. Invariably it either means to scroll down on a spreadsheet or when a column is filtered to drill down until you find what you want. It doesn't mean to start drilling into the concrete and perform deep excavation. But you would be forgiven for thinking that.

25. I'll do a high level (helicopter)review

High level reviews and summaries are commonplace in offices today. Senior managers and executives don't necessarily need to know the detail and intricate nature of some reports. They will instead ask for a summary of the main points, normally referred to as a high level summary. If a document has been reviewed already a high level review may be needed. A quick scan through is performed to see if there are any mistakes that have not been spotted. On occasion a high level review can be described as a helicopter review. I will admit I have only heard one person use the term helicopter review but it means the same as high level. So if anyone asks you to do a high level review they don't mean running to the top of the building and performing a review, it is basically a quick scan of a document or report that has been reviewed already.

26. Have you checked with "the business"?

We all work in certain departments, whether they be finance, sales, information technology, human resources or customer service. When reviews of processes or workflows are being carried out with the intention of improving procedures and lowering costs, the remainder of the company apart from your department tends to be described as "*the business*". I for one found the term a little confusing to grasp, as "*the business*" could quite conceivably mean anything.

Context is important when using this term. A scenario could happen that you have been tasked with improving the relationship between two departments in the company. You come up with proposals to improve this relationship. When you report them to your line manager the question may arise, how do your proposals affect the business? What is done in one department may have a knock on effect in another. This is one context the phrase could be used. The phrase is too generic for my liking but very common.

27. You got to pull your weight

This is an old fashioned phrase that has been used in all types of work situations. I don't hear it used that often anymore. Its meaning is self explanatory. If an employee or colleague is not doing their job adequately or not meeting the necessary targets set by superiors then they might be asked to pull their weight more. Simply their performance levels need to improve.

28. I'm leaving a sinking ship

A few years ago a colleague of mine left is job. I asked why he was leaving and he replied by saying he felt his employer didn't listen to his views anymore on certain topics and also that he felt it was the right time to leave a sinking ship. The ship in question was a well known financial institution that had hit bad times primarily because of the recession an also bad decision making. The phrase has been around for a long time but the context has remained the same. It simply means leaving a company or job that you feel you have no future in. The prime reason being you think the industry or company you work for is in a downward spiral or economic trouble. Leaving a sinking ship may be the right or easy thing to do but time will only tell if the ship does actually sink.

29. He is a good networker

The literal meaning of this phrase is that someone is a good communicator, possibly extroverted, charismatic and charming. They like to interact and make professional contacts. They network well. I have always felt that the phrase "*he is a good networker*" has a hidden meaning in certain contexts. It can on occasion mean that someone has got to a position of authority by his network of contacts and not necessarily by his experience and knowledge. The old adage of it's who you know and not what you know rings true here. Maybe it's the cynic in me but I do feel that people who are described as good networkers are essentially full of hot air and nonsense.

30. He's got his fingers in a lot of pies

This phrase has a comedic element to it and again has been used in many contexts. At its basic level it simply means that someone has an interest or stake in a lot of companies (possibly financially) or has conducted many business deals with different individuals. They are risk takers and adventurous by nature and like to dabble in many projects. Venture capitalists could be said to have their fingers in many pies if they have invested in many businesses whether small or large.

The comedic element to the phrase tends to come from film and theatre where the phrase can often have a dodgy undercurrent to it. It can mean someone has a seedy character and gets involved in a string of immoral or illegal activities. Delboy from Only Fools and Horses (the famous BBC sitcom from 1980s and 90s) could be said to have had his fingers in a lot of pies. A small time businessman whose business dealings could be best described as dodgy.

31. There has been a paradigm shift

It is unusual to hear this phrase but it has become slightly more popular of late. It mostly means that plans around something such as a new procedure or new system being implemented have changed dramatically. The "*paradigm shift*" has meant the current plans have changed and the team or employees concerned will need to be advised on the new developments. It may be used in different contexts but the meaning invariably always stays the same. A new management team or CEO could bring in new dynamics and a new way of thinking that could be described as a *"paradigm shift"* compared to a previous regime.

32. Going forward

When a task or process is completed incompetently or just not to the requisite level then improvements are made. These new processes and procedures will need to be implemented. Invariably the phrase *"going forward"* will be used in this context. A manager may say *"going forward"* can the following task be done this way. The phrase is quite generic and not explicit enough. The term can cause confusion as it doesn't come with a prescribed date, therefore *"going forward"* can literally mean anything.

33. I'm snowed under and I'm flat out

Both these phrases mean roughly the same thing. The old favourite of *"I'm snowed under"* is used as much today as it was it times gone by. It still conveys a message of someone who is very busy. *"I'm flat out"* can mean you are busy just with one task whereas *"I'm snowed under"* can imply a greater level of stress and workload. From my own experience *"I'm flat out"* is used more predominantly now in the modern office. It can also sometimes be used to give the impression that you are working to your capacity when it fact you just don't want to take on any extra responsibility or work.

34. You're not a team player

I have heard this phrase so often over the past thirteen years; both directly and indirectly that it has lost its meaning. Managers and superiors tend use this phrase to belittle and talk in a condescending manner to colleagues. They will imply *"you are not a team player"* when the proof of this is negligible. In fact it is a manager and team leader's responsibility to build a team that embodies collaboration, good work ethics and team spirit. Managers have to understand that each individual has a different working style and they need to embrace these styles, not ostracise employees for them.

Quite simply some employees like working independently and some prefer increased interaction with their team during work tasks and actions. The bottom line is once the required tasks get done and done correctly that's what matters. To imply someone is not a team player is in my opinion bad management. It reflects badly on the manager concerned. We all work in teams, but we all have different ways of doing this. There are many different personality traits. A manager needs to recognise this fact and make a team gel accordingly. If for any reason an employee breaches company policies on team ethics or terms of their employment contracts, then by all means these employees should be reprimanded. But stating an employee is not a team player without foundation is shameful. It can be a form of bullying.

35. It's been a crazy day (I'm run off my feet)

Literally this phrase implies it's been a very busy working day. From my own experience employees who tend not to be used to the rigours of hard work blurt this phrase out after a few hours of increased workload. The reality is not every day is crazy when it comes to working in an office. Most days might be busy, this is normal, but rarely to working days become crazy that the phrase needs to be used on a consistent or recurring basis. *"I'm run off my feet"* is more reflective of a working day when one has possibly not been able to take lunch or has had lunch on the go. I personally prefer someone saying this as it gives the impression of a tiring work day whether this is true or not.

36. I've been stuck in meetings all day

A previous manager I worked for used say this phrase nearly every evening around 5pm. She would have spent most of her day attending meetings, the majority organised by her to fill the day. When she would return to her desk in the late afternoon, she would say the phrase loud enough for everyone on the team to hear. What she was trying to do was imply that she had been too busy with meetings all day that she couldn't carry out her routine daily tasks. These tasks would then be delegated to other team members causing them to get delayed in work. Whilst some employees will genuinely be stuck in meetings through no fault of their own, organising meetings of no consequence or value to fill the day is ethically wrong. So while the literal meaning may be simple the actual meaning can deviate away from that.

37. Did you get sign off?

An old favourite and a continuously used phrase on the office floor is *"did you get sign off?"* It is used when reports or documents need signing or if new procedures and processes are being introduced. A line manager or employee responsible will ask if this particular item has been signed off by the appropriate signatory in the office, whether this is senior management or a project manager. In a world of compliance and checklists every little item needs to be signed off before it is ready for introduction or to be sent to a client. This is part of the joys of modern day office life.

38. When will that be rolled out? / When is it going live?

When any new system is developed there will be a timescale in place for it to be introduced to the office. It could be introduced in a pilot, phased, parallel or big bang approach. Whatever method is chosen the phrases above are used to describe a launch date for the system. Employees will ask *"when is it going live?"* or *"when will it be rolled out?"* They both mean the same thing. The phrase can also be used when launching new processes and procedures, it all depends on the context.

39. You got to start towing the line

The above phrase is not unique to the modern day office. It is dying out in its use but can still be heard being used by certain individuals. It means that one needs to get in line with company policies and not be deviating away from what is perceived as company norms when it comes to working. If managers or employees methods are archaic or are perceived to be a detriment to the good of the company then authority may need to be questioned on this.

Without continuous change and improvement work processes and procedures will not move with the times. In this context if you are asked *"to start towing the line"* it may be appropriate to challenge this approach. If you are correctly being asked *"to tow the line"* as you are being disruptive and are possibly in breach of your employment terms then it may be advisable *"to start towing the line"*, whatever this line may be.

40. Let's have a chat

This phrase is very similar to *"let's have a catch up"*. Whilst this phrase seems straight forward, in my own experience it can have a hidden meaning and negative connotations. A manager or superior may come over to you or send an email stating they want to have a chat. It may seem inconsequential or innocuous but *"let's have a chat"* could mean they want to break bad news to you. A manager may say weekend work or overtime is needed. Annual leave that has been requested may be refused or a task may not have been completed to the satisfaction of your manager. Worse still it could mean you are being made redundant or your contract is not being renewed.

The use of the phrase is subjective, but once heard it probably means you will be taken away to a small meeting room and informed of bad news. If you are lucky it might be positive news, a promotion or pay rise. Another form of *"let's have a chat"* is stating you would like to have a 1:1 meeting. Again this tends to mean the same thing, but slightly more formal.

41. It's on my radar

I would be surprised if you haven't heard someone use this in the office. It's commonly used in phone conversations when one colleague to another will state that a work process or task that needs to be completed is in his work plan or diary for the coming hours or days. Essentially it means that you haven't forgotten about doing something and you are letting someone else know (possibly a superior) that this task *"is on your radar"*. Outside the office the context of using the phrase *"it's on my radar"* means something different altogether. It can refer to fighter jets or airplanes being watched on radar screens by air traffic control, or intelligence agencies and even NASA.

42. I'll touch base with you later

Quite simply this means that you will call or email a colleague later on in the day or week to update them on how a particular work task is progressing. It's a friendly way of saying you'll see if everything is ok and if any help is needed later on regarding the task in question. In critical deadline driven business environments it can be used to make sure tasks are on track and no delays will occur that will impact clients.

43. I'll get the ball rolling on this

This tends to relate to new projects or plans of action regarding tasks and processes that need to get started. A colleague will state "*I'll get the ball rolling on this*" when possibly talking to his manager on the phone regarding the issue. Whether this ball keeps rolling until the completion of the project is another matter entirely. This phrase tends to be heard with frequent regularity on the office floor.

44. Can you roll this forward

This invariably means can you update a report or excel spreadsheet so that it includes this month's data instead of last months. Essentially using up to date data to "*roll forward*" previous information. It can mean the partial or full update of information. It is commonly heard in deadline driven businesses who report daily, weekly and monthly. When I worked in the funds industry it was heard on the hour every hour. It became a daily ritual.

45. I'll chase up on this

This is a typical phrase that tends to be heard in numerous phone conversations daily. With the vast array of work employees undertake in their day to day roles certain tasks will get forgotten about or put to one side. After a certain period of time if a task or process has not been completed a colleague will normally enquirer as to the status of this aforementioned task. It may be that you need an update from another office or you are waiting on another colleague to complete the task. At this stage you may be asked by a manager or superior to chase up on this. It is used regularly on the office floor and in varying contexts.

46. Is there a process in place for this?

This phrase seems to be the default option when a process fails or if no process is in place for a certain task or workflow. A possible safety valve or a phrase uttered as a means to relieve anxiety in certain situations. Undoubtedly if a process is not in place it soon will be after this phrase is said.

47. I can't make head nor tail of what you did!

This phrase is common in most walks of life and is seldom heard on the office floor. However during my time working professionally I have heard it's stated over phone conversations or when discussing work or tasks already completed. It is not the best way to converse with a colleague when you might not understand what has been done and this may be an explanation as to why it has virtually disappeared off the office floor.

48. Put it on the back-burner

If a task needs to be done but isn't deemed that important it may be put on the back burner. That is simply it has been dropped down the list of priorities and will be picked up some time in the future.

49. Was this not raised before?

This tends to be stated when an important error or omission is noticed. To relieve anxiety or to pass the blame a worker will state has this issue not been raised before. The context it is used is important but my experience is that this phrase is used to try and apportion blame on to some other colleague.

50. Switch it on and off (when your PC crashes)

It's happened to us all, our computer crashes and we think there is something highly technical wrong and ring the information technology service desk. Invariably their first port of call is to ask you to switch your pc on and off. To be fair this normally solves the problem but it tends to be an overly used default mechanism for service desk staff. In fact it is probably easier not to ring the service desk and switch the pc on and off yourself; this may save you time and heartache.

Chapter 3

The Office Bully

Introduction

For the first ten years of my working life I never gave a second thought to the issue of workplace bullying or for that matter had heard many instances of it occurring. When we think of bullying we often think of the child in schoolyard being called names or the teenager being harassed and picked on by class mates.

Modern technology has made bullying more prevalent and helped the bully come up with more cunning and devious ways in which to inflict physical and psychological pain on the individuals being bullied. Texting and e-mails can be used to bully. Certain social media sites like Ask FM or even Facebook have become the new platforms to inflict unwanted abuse on innocent victims. There is no denying that bullying of this nature goes on and that it is a huge problem in modern society. Recent cases over the last few years of tragic teenage suicides relating to direct bullying has highlighted this.

But what happens when kids grow up and enter the workforce. Does bullying stop? Does the bully not exist in the workplace? You would think so as very little is heard of workplace bullying, especially in the UK and Ireland, whereas in countries like the USA and Australia more attention is given to this ugly part of organisational culture. Companies want this type of bullying brushed under the carpet and they will never admit it occurs. The stress that people feel in their jobs is growing and in some instances has reached boiling point.

Heavy workloads, fear of redundancy and an ever lingering economic recession that is slowly disappearing has seen workplace bullying increase. When I hear either directly or indirectly that someone is off sick indefinitely, I think to myself is that due to workplace bullying? It's hard to quantify how prevalent bullying is but there is no doubt it goes on. I always used to think that talk of bullying in workplaces was nonsense and that work was work, and we just got on with it. But what if you were the victim of bullying yourself? Your mindset and views would quickly change. How would you cope with that situation? It's too hard to know until you are unlucky enough to come face to face with the modern office bully.

So what is workplace bullying?

It's been a grey area for companies in years gone by. It wasn't easy to describe or give an accurate explanation of, but modern society is more appreciative of the fact that it does exist and in some industries is widespread. In Ireland back in 2007, an ERSI (The Economic and Social Research Institute) survey on workplace bullying defined it as *"repeated inappropriate behaviour, direct or indirect, whether verbal, physical or otherwise, conducted by one or more persons against another or others, at the place of work and /or in the course of employment, which could reasonably be regarded as undermining the individual's right to dignity at work"* This definition is a little vague and can be interpreted in different ways but another body in Ireland, the Health and Safety Authority, went further and gave examples of behaviour that could constitute bullying. These included purposely undermining someone, targeting someone for special negative treatment, social exclusion or isolation, intimidation, aggressive or obscene language and repeated requests for the completion of tasks with unreasonable deadlines or the completion of impossible tasks. While all the mentioned points are valid, the latter is significant. Think to yourself, how many times have you been given impossible tasks to do with ridiculous deadlines attached to these? Has this occurred more than once? Even once is an issue, but if it's been occurring regularly (continuous and more than once) for a sustained period of time there is no question you are being bullied. Unrealistic demands of employees are not to be tolerated anymore. But the fear is employees will just put up with it as they don't want to lose their jobs (especially in a recession), or that no one will believe them or take them seriously if they report the incident to a higher internal authority.

The Workplace Bullying Institute in the USA defined bullying as repeated health harming behaviours that can include verbal abuse, offensive conduct and intentional sabotage. The important word here is health and the damage such mentioned behaviour does to your health.

The sly and vindictive bully

About two years ago a friend of mine said he was out of work sick. He didn't mention why and I just said I hope you are better soon. Six months down the line we were talking again and he said he had gone back to work but that in total he was out sick for three months. He felt a little coy and embarrassed about telling me why he was sick. He looked physically fine so I knew it had to be psychological and stress related. He told me he had been working late in work, doing crazy hours for about two years and that his manager was an overbearing, nasty piece of work. I asked him to explain and elaborate further. He mentioned he was being harassed by his manager, being asked to perform multiple tasks each day that went far beyond his remit. Other members of the team were being let get away with doing next to nothing yet my friend had to work late hours without pay and lunch for days on end. He received no thanks and was constantly told that his performance was under par. Most of this was done through e-mail, the modern medium for subtle harassment. All the working late hours and mental torture from his manager took its toll on his family life and eventually something had to give. He went to his doctor one morning and explained that he could not face going into work anymore and that it had now become a nightmare. The doctor didn't take long to realise that my friend was completely stressed and mentally drained. The company had forced him into taking drastic measures. He had reached the point of no return, that is he could not face the office again.

After three months away from the office and feeling refreshed and reinvigorated my friend decided it was time to go back to work. His manager had been made aware of the situation and my friend who we will call Michael went back to work in a different team to the one he worked in previously. All was going well for about nine months, work was tough but he was getting home at 6pm everyday and there was no working late nights. Then without warning he was asked to return back to his old team and to work for his old boss. He said to his current manager that this was not a good idea and that he would prefer not to go back working for the old manager. His pleas were ignored and ultimately he ended back in the same situation working long hours and taking grief from his manager. Work was the same as before and he asked his manager for a meeting to discuss his workload. He asked politely could some deadlines be put back a few days to give him extra time to work through the backlog as he was working every hour that god sent. The manager agreed to his request but almost immediately once the meeting was finished sent him an e-mail stating that the deadlines were being brought forward by two days. This was outrageous and only enraged Michael.

Other accusations were beginning to be thrown at him. He was accused of security breaches; the accusations were lame at this stage. The final straw though, came when he could not get out of work on time after he made it clear that his child's birthday was on one evening. He returned to the doctor who was shocked by the latest developments and quickly diagnosed work related stress. When I heard this story I was obviously appalled. I took a step back and thought about exactly what my friend was going through, it had all the hallmarks of workplace bullying. It made me sick to think companies are behaving in this manner and that nothing is being done about it. When I finished talking to Michael I realised I had never asked him was his manager a man or a woman. I had a fair idea of what sex the bully was. Can you guess? It was an old fashioned way of management I thought. Bullying through heavy workloads, using power and control, sly and snide remarks and using e-mail as a forum of attack.

I am no psychologist, I just have a keen interest in it, but it wasn't too hard for me to figure this out. Yes you might have guessed it by now, it was a woman who was my friends' manager and a bully. Now not all bullies are women, in fact most are men, but bullying of a psychological nature tends to be perpetrated by women in the workplace. Women are less likely to be a physical bully. Male bullying is more open and apparent to other colleagues. It can be more verbal, tactile and physical. Whereas women tend to be more cunning and secretive about whom they target. They use their position to target what they perceive as possibly weak individuals who won't fight back. Only a small percentage of women (though increasing) bully other colleagues in the workplace but when they do it is vindictive and highly effective and can lead to mental anguish and high stress for the victim.

The sad thing about Michael's story is that individuals in a position of authority and the human resource department knew exactly what was going on and who the perpetrators were. Yet they decided to play a waiting game hoping to force Michael to resign and ultimately wishing to brush this sorry episode under the carpet. They didn't seem to realise how detrimental what they were doing was to Michael's health and to the company's reputation. On the face of it they simply didn't care. Eventually Michael left his position within the company but this was only after his legal team agreed a settlement with the company for damages relating to the stress and anguish he suffered. They never admitted liability and Michael officially had been made redundant. But I knew and everyone associated with this sad case knew that bullying was the prime reason behind Michael leaving his job.

My story – A tale of institutional bullying

Amazingly even after what my friend Michael had told me, I still didn't think bullying was a huge issue in the workplace. I was a little naive as to the prevalence of this sensitive issue. But my thoughts were soon to change. Soon afterwards I started a new job and became the victim of psychological bullying from not just one but two women and a senior manager who was male. Yes three superiors were bullying me simultaneously, a horrible situation to be in.

Unfortunately in the times we live people think they can get away with bullying for a number of reasons, the victim might fear there is no way out, as the jobs market is condensed and tightened in a recession. Human resource managers are on the whole not independent and the victim might think they will not get a fair hearing if they issue a complaint. Possibly most importantly senior managers and executives seem oblivious to the fact that workplace bullying is a huge problem and only getting worse. They prefer for instances of bullying to be put to one side and don't view them as an issue. If it doesn't affect the bottom line why should they care? Well that is a dangerous game to play, as in the end everything affects the bottom line, even bullying. No company wants to end up with a reputation for bullying. Business is global now and reputations count for everything. Being green and having a healthy work environment was a huge seller in last fifteen to twenty years. Companies embraced these green philosophies. Now companies need to take a real look at workplace bullying and stamp it out. Companies can't ignore this problem any longer. Can companies afford to pay out to individuals who win cases relating to workplace stress and bullying? I don't think so. Preventative measures are crucial. Below is what I encountered when I started a new job in a well known and powerful company in the financial services sector. It is told in a case study format as I decided to document as much information as possible when I realised I was becoming the victim of office bullying.

Billy Connolly once said on a TV interview with Michael Parkinson in 1980, that when he was on stage performing in Washington DC in America, that the audience made him feel *"as welcome as a fart in a spacesuit"*. He thought they were there to see Elton John, not himself. When I heard this first I found it extremely humorous and crude of course. It was only when I had been working in a company in the financial services sector for a little over two months that I thought to myself, that I have never felt welcome here and the management have done little or nothing to make me feel at home. That is when I remembered Billy Connolly's quote above.

Although the quote may be a bit rude and not wholly appropriate, it is extremely funny. The fact is I did feel about as welcome as fart in a spacesuit in this particular company. I remembered thinking, what have I done to deserve this? I pondered over this for a few days and came to the conclusion that I had done absolutely nothing wrong and in fact was doing my job to a high level. I had received numerous talks by the manager about my performance, saying I needed to up my game and now it was time to step up to the mark. I was bewildered with these mini reviews as I felt they were totally unnecessary. The style of management I was encountering in this particular company was archaic at best.

Whilst I agree and acknowledge any ones performance levels could approve, I had only just joined the company and to make things even stranger the manager had pursued me on numerous occasions to make sure I was actually starting on the day that I had agreed to start. I had received at least three phone calls in the prior two weeks before I commenced employment by my future manager to confirm that I would definitely be starting. It definitely was a little overbearing but in hindsight a sign of this woman's controlling personality. I thought it a little odd but still went ahead with the job offer. I had agreed to start and decided to stick by my word. Unfortunately the first two months in this company was only the beginning of a nightmare eight months before I decided enough was enough and moved on.

I had taken the role in good faith and wanted to improve my experience in my current field of expertise. It seemed like a good role and an opportunity to advance. The interview for the job was tough, a competence based interview where numerous questions were asked about my technical skills and knowledge. Very few questions were asked on my people skills, how I dealt with internal or external clients. This was normally a standard interview question, but I guess they didn't view this as important. And I was soon to find out that this companies people management and soft skills were appalling.

The two managers interviewing me seemed normal, one was extremely quiet (my future manager) and the other was a bit more forceful in her line of questioning. I thought this was the manager I would be potentially working for. The interview lasted an hour, quite standard fair and when finished, I thought this job is in the bag. The following week I got offered the job and after a day to mull it over I decided I would take it. The jobs market was tight and I honestly thought this might be a good opportunity, something a little different.

The company had made headline news for all the wrong reasons in the previous years and I became a little nervous about starting there. I wasn't sure if I was making the right decision, something felt wrong but I had signed a contract and would honour it. Ireland was still a country in a deep recession and any job was good, wasn't it?

The first few weeks in the job were quiet, I hadn't access to systems yet and therefore the work I was doing was administration based. The job description had stated I would be working at the heart of the reporting team learning new processes and that I would be allowed to make an impact on the team. What was not mentioned to me before I started was that I would be reporting to two managers in a group of six employees and also that I would have a head of finance overlook my every move in the company.

From week five onwards everything changed, I had just returned from the Christmas break and I felt like I was now being constantly watched. Were they expecting me to show my abilities, maybe so? I had no access to any systems still and hadn't been shown what they wanted me to do. I was sitting at my desk with vast amounts of expertise, literally being left to rot. I was also beginning to be micro-managed by one of the managers and after six weeks there was no sign of any accounting or reporting work, it was all mundane spreadsheet and administration work. Had I accepted a different job, I wondered? Was the job description a lie? Or simply had I made a huge error of judgement in accepting the job? Was my gut instinct right? These questions raced through my mind.

The team I worked in was summoned to a meeting one morning and the manager stated that she had been working crazy hours, doing overtime until 11 and 12pm for the past week. I was shocked, and thought what on earth have you been doing working to that time. She gave her speech demanding we all improve our effort and stating that the reason for her late hours was that the work we hadn't done had filtered down to her and she had do it. I could not understand her reasoning; we had never been told in the team of extra work going or even if this work could have been done in our core working hours. She demanded we work late that night and get critical client based work finished. I stayed until 6.30pm and finished my tasks and thought if this work had been delegated out more efficiently it could have been done sooner and in the previous days. I knew now that the management skills of my manager were suspect to say the least. She seemed to blame others for her failings of management including poor delegation of tasks.

I was now eight weeks into my new job, I definitely didn't feel settled but was still keen to make an impact and succeed. I received an e-mail from my manager saying she wanted to have a short meeting about my progress to date. I accepted the request and didn't think too much about it. It seemed a little strange to be having another meeting about progress when I wasn't in the company a wet week and didn't have access to the accounting system. Maybe I was wrong but I thought it was up to the company you joined to provide access to an operational system.

The short meeting took place in the canteen, I was told under no uncertain terms that I needed to improve my work and it was now time to show what I was about. I didn't take too much notice of the meeting, I thought the manager was a little intense and odd but just thought to myself, maybe this is the style of management that operates in the company.

Roll forward another week and I was now over two months in the company. I had been told that I was to report to my team leader who in turn would report to the manager. I was never told of this when I accepted the job, I was under the assumption that I would report to one manager and have more dealings with the reporting and accounting function of the team. It appeared I had been lied to.

My team leader had at best poor people skills. She seemed socially challenged and basic conversations and interactions were awkward. Her style was micro-management and a management based on mistrust. She simply didn't trust anyone to do the jobs she had asked them to carry out and because of this; she constantly looked over the shoulder of people and didn't let them get on with their work. I was constantly asked when something was done and if I was ok performing mundane and basic tasks. Her controlling nature meant working for her was going to be difficult and a challenge but it was a challenge I wanted to succeed at. I had never worked for a micro-manager and someone who could not delegate anything at all on their task list.

I knew her poor people skills could be a problem. She was very abrasive and abrupt in her manner and demanded things were done rather than asking in a civil and polite way. On one afternoon in late January things blew up. It had been a very busy day and it was 4.30pm and I was looking forward to going home, one of those days. She asked me could I help out another team with a task and I said I would. A few minutes later a member of the other team came over and said in front of me and my team leader that he was free now and no longer needed my assistance. I said ok and my team leader agreed. At 4.55pm an e-mail was sent to my team leader saying the task was still not completed and that it was now urgent. Without warning she roared at me and asked why the task wasn't done. I was a little shocked as no one had roared at me in ten years of business, well not on an office floor, and not in front of the floor staff. It was simply unprofessional and unexpected. I said that the other team member stated he would complete the task (of which she knew) and there had obviously been a misunderstanding or miscommunication. She immediately summoned be into a meeting room and told me under no uncertain terms that I was to do what I was told without question.

It seemed like I was working for a dictator now, not a team leader. I went back to my desk shocked, as even though I am a fully grown man well capable of standing up for myself, I had never been spoken to in that manner by anyone in a work situation before. I thought to myself, that behaviour was totally unacceptable and out of order. How dare she speak to me like that, I was angry and fuming, boiling up with pure frustration. I completed the task within twenty minutes, it wasn't that important and could have waited until the following morning, but if it pleased my team leader I would get it done.

I went home that night and thought about what had happened. I came to the conclusion that what had happened was disgraceful and that I needed to have a word with my team leader about this. I e-mailed her the next morning requesting a short meeting. I told her that what she had done the previous afternoon was wrong and that I wanted an apology. She blatantly refused and turned the tables totally back at me stating that I was uncooperative and didn't take direction well. I thought this response was weak, but I was not surprised. Like most bullies she refused to acknowledge she was doing anything wrong. I thought after the short meeting that it was going to be difficult to work with my team leader going forward but I was a professional worker and would do my best to work with her in a polite and cordial way. So for the rest of the day I did my duties and was civil to my team leader and thought to myself maybe this will blow over and that she had had a bad afternoon. I gave her the benefit of the doubt.

The next day I returned into work and to my shock and utter amazement I saw a request to attend a meeting by the head of finance and another manager at 11am. I was bewildered by this and knew it couldn't be good. What had I done I thought? My team leader had obviously escalated what had happened the previous day to a higher level. Maybe she felt what I had said was inappropriate. To me she was just staying one step ahead of the game and covering her tracks. I knew I had done nothing wrong but as in most companies the powers that be maybe wanted to make a point of who was boss. Even now I was beginning to think this was becoming more like bullying. I decided I would go to the meeting at 11am, be calm, say little or nothing and listen to what was being said. When I entered the meeting room, the head of finance immediately started to accuse me of being passive, lacking initiative, having a poor attitude and he questioned why I was working in the company. He stated, do you want to be here? I said yes of course I want to be here. I took this job in good faith and would like to do my job (or as I thought in my head be left ALONE to do my job). I stated I was happy in the company but not happy with what had happened the previous afternoon with my team leader.

He dismissed my concerns and didn't listen to me when I stated what my team leader had done was wrong. This was inconsequential to him. Who was I to question his authority in any manner? It was like the catholic church, there was an old school mentality of never to question authority and just take your punishment whatever it was.

He started to focus on who I was speaking to and getting on with in the company (within my department) and mentioned three colleagues. He reminded me that these people were not management and that I had to get along with management too. I agreed and said I always endeavour to get along with management but that what had happened with my team leader was disgraceful. Was he indirectly trying to stop me talking to certain colleagues in the team, it was hard to know but my guess was this was the case. He stated that I had now issues with three levels of management, but I knew the truth was that they had issues with me, not the other way around. I was astounded now and wasn't completely sure what was going on.

I was now being accused of being passive, unhappy, and not able to get on with management and also of not wanting to work for the company. I felt like I was being psycho analysed and to make things worse the head of finance had brought back-up into the room in the form of a manager from another team. I was of course on my own so it felt like more bullying, two against one culture. I was given a stark ultimatum, to go home and decide if I wanted to work for the company. I had to come back the following day and state whether I would start a fresh in the company and forget about what had happened, so in essence, forget that I had been roared at by my team leader for no apparent reason and forget the small but reoccurring instances of bullying or take the easy way out and hand in my notice and get one month's pay and part company.

I totally disagreed with what was going on, I was simply being forced into making a decision and been told to forget about the events that had happened in the previous days and weeks. Although I didn't like it and felt frustrated and a little helpless I decided to stay. My reasoning was that I had done nothing wrong. I was the person wronged. The whole saga had a strong smell of bullying about it, but I was a little unsure what to do. I hadn't found myself in this situation before in previous jobs and I felt isolated. Did they simply not like me and wanted me to leave or was it something deeper? Could they not see the faults of the team leader or was it a case of that she is in a higher position and can get away with this. I discussed my thoughts with colleagues and they all agreed that the actions of the previous few days had all the hallmarks of bullying. The question now was what would or could I do?

I was only two and half months into a new job and had agreed to give it a go. Should I bite my lip and simply grin and bear it until at least a year had been done or maybe go to HR and put a written complaint in. But HR was not independent and the chances were they will always side with management. They held all the cards. I decided to take some time to reflect on what happened, but work had become unbearable. I felt I was being forced out of the company; it wasn't a nice feeling, one I wouldn't wish on anyone. If I stayed the micro management and bullying would probably continue. It looked like I was doomed as something would eventually have to give. I decided to give it at least six months and see if things would improve. It was February and I had started in November so I didn't want to leave a job after only three months. This wasn't me and I didn't want to give up so easily. I had an exam in late May and had decided to go to night classes to help with my study and preparation. It would give me something to take my mind off work and focus on.

Back in December my wife had given birth to our first child, a beautiful baby girl so family life was hectic but enjoyable. I was getting little sleep as one does when a new child is born but by

February I had definitely adjusted to the reduced sleeping time. I was thinking to myself, am I tired and on edge all the time because I have a new baby at home or is it work. My conclusion was always that it was work. This was a no brainer. After three months in the job I was starting to get mentally fatigued and exhausted by the bullying tactics of the management team. I felt I was not being given a fair chance.

March came and things in work had calmed down a little, there was still the constant micro management but I was slowly beginning to settle into the job. It was hard; don't get me wrong, coming in every morning and having over twenty five e-mails (sent by my team leader) in my inbox was hard to deal with. My days were being filled by mundane administration tasks, but I was getting through it admirably. It wasn't the accounting job I was promised and interviewed for, but it was job and I was willing to do it in the short term. I was realistic, the country is in a recession and being employed was a good thing. It did feel like I was drowning slowly, trying to keep my head above water, but what else could I do? The jobs market was poor.

My team leader was in her mid forties, maybe fifty, it was hard to tell, but she had over twenty years experience of working. From speaking to colleagues who had known her previously or who knew people who worked with her, I found out that she was extremely intense and had very poor people skills. She was renowned for working crazy late hours. Her working day was 7am to 12am midnight, not a normal 9am to 5pm day that most people did. It would be hard to compete with this, as I had a family now at home and at best could work the odd hour of overtime here and there. The month of March was going along smoothly, our team was preparing for the accounting year end that fell at 31st March. It was very busy, I was being bombarded by e-mail after e-mail, some sent past midnight. My work ethic had always been to get your work done, make sure it's of good quality and go home and enjoy yourself. Work hard and play hard. But it looked like I had joined a company and an organisational culture that promoted long hours and had very little time for the concept of a work life balance. If I arrived into work at 9.05am I was reprimanded for being late and not ringing ahead. This behaviour and style of management was pathetic, pedantic and a bad reflection on her as a person.

It was coming to the end of March; the bullying seemed to have subsided. Micro management was still the norm but I had begun to get used to this. Admittedly it had been hard to do. I came into the office one morning and saw a meeting request with my manager. It was set for 11am and I was under the illusion that it was another mini review of my work for the previous two months so I prepared accordingly. However when I entered the meeting room, my manager proceeded to talk about how busy we were and were going to be in the coming months. I thought to myself, what is this about. She said that members of the team, basically herself and my team leader were working crazy hours and that it was essential everyone work overtime over the next four to six weeks. She said there would be a lot of weekend work ahead and that I was needed in and that there was no discussion on the matter. I paused for a second and composed my thoughts and replied stating that I was prepared to come in on some Saturdays once I obviously was being paid overtime. She immediately replied stating no one gets paid overtime. I knew this was a lie; of course employees in the company got paid overtime. Maybe not all but definitely some were. I said I was only prepared to work overtime once I got paid. She explicitly said this was not possible and because I wanted to help the team I said I would work until 7 or 7.30pm on some nights if it was needed. I knew this would be unpaid work but I was prepared to help the team out. When I put this suggestion forward it was dismissed and I was accused of not putting the team first. I said I was of course a team player but my number one team was at home and I had to always put them first. My manager looked at me like I had two heads. Had I offended her? I think not but she didn't like my response that was for sure. Her work ethic was simple. You either work here until 11 or 12pm every night or come in at the weekends or you're not welcome in my team. This was madness as far as I was concerned. Just as I thought the bullying had subsided from my team leader, back came my manager with more.

What value would I get out of working overtime and not getting paid? And working weekends and not getting paid a cent was insane. Give up valuable family life for nothing, I don't think so. Maybe over three months of bullying and harassment had made me think like this, but I didn't think I was wrong. After ten minutes in the meeting my manager stated clearly she thought I wasn't a team player and was showing no commitment to the team and company. After all I was on a short term contract, what commitment was the company showing to me? I had taken the job in good faith and for over four months had been subjected to ongoing bullying that now was showing no signs of stopping. I totally disagreed with my manager's assessment; I was without question committed to the team. If they let me show this they would see, but they were intent at this stage of forcing me out. I had come to this conclusion now. My manager finished the meeting by ignoring me and walking out of the meeting room. Very professional I thought to myself. She was like a spoiled schoolchild who just didn't get her way and this lady was over fifty. An old school bully who loved what she did. The company didn't care though. They knew she was a bully but the toxic culture that prevailed in the company endorsed bullying.

I still didn't want to just get up and leave the company, why should I? I talked to a colleague who now was working in a different team in the company but had previously worked in my current team under my manager. He told me without hesitation that she was very difficult to work for and that seventeen employees had gone through this team in the previous two years. They had either moved on internally or externally and the common denominator in those previous two years was my current manager. It didn't take a genius to figure out that my manager wasn't exactly the best manager that had ever walked the planet. She was the primary reason why people were leaving. Surely people of a higher standing in the company had noticed this trend, sure it was staring them in the face. The question was, were they prepared to do anything about it? It didn't seem likely. My manager was never the most pleasant person to deal with; I noticed that from day one. She would barely say hello to me in the mornings and to be honest she didn't say hello at all. This was pure basics of people management and she simply didn't understand this. To be fair I didn't mind it, I preferred if she didn't talk to me at all, but the bullying just magnified everything. So now I had dealt with at least three instances in my first few months in the job where I felt I had been bullied. My team leader and manager were bullies, no doubt about that now. What next I thought, could it get worse, you bet it could.

If this had been my first job out of college I might have thought that the behaviour of my managers was normal and to be expected in any company. But I had over ten years experience and I had worked in many companies at this stage and I had never experienced bullying tactics like this before. I was always never completely sure if I was being bullied, it's hard to be completely sure of this. But having my feelings and thoughts reinforced by colleagues confirmed to me that this was definitely bullying. It wasn't the physical bullying you might find in the school playground or second level schools; it was more controlling and psychological bullying. My team leader and manager were control freaks, who liked dominating employees and controlling every thought and move they made. Their superiors in the company had never reprimanded them for this and hence they believed their actions were normal and a correct way of managing. In fact their style of management was not just archaic, it's harmful to the company, work production and processes suffer and more importantly it's a form of psychological bullying and torture on the employee who is in the firing line. It's not acceptable in modern day businesses.

It was the start of April now and going to work every Monday was uncomfortable and demoralising. My life was hell in this company and the only thing keeping me going was my family and making sure I provide for them. But I knew mentally and physically I couldn't take too much more of this. My patience was running out. I still didn't believe that going to HR was an option as a HR department in an old style company like this was of no use to me. Their independence was compromised. Why would they support an employee in an operational role? I wanted to stay at least six months, this was my target, and it wasn't far off now. Once that target was achieved I would start looking for another job. Life was too short to be dealing with constant bullying every day. I was definitely stressed and even though I didn't see it, it was now affecting my health and home life.

The month of April passed off with little incidence. I was getting to know my colleagues a little better. My team leader was still enforcing her world of micro management. Every morning I would see the obligatory twenty e-mails plus in my in-box with numerous administration tasks assigned but I didn't care anymore. She would come over to me before I had even switched on my computer dictating what needed to be done and what the priorities were for the day. Every five minutes I was checked up on and I felt like a three year old in playschool. But this was a bad reflection on her, not me.

There was no doubt I was going to leave the job but the reality was that I could be here for a while, even another year so I had decided that I would keep my head down and get on with the work to the best of my ability.

I had booked a holiday in early February, sending the e-mail request to my team leader and manager. I was due to take the last week of May off. I had an exam on the Wednesday of that week so I wanted time off to do some study and then once the exam was over go on a small family holiday to de-stress and unwind. I was looking forward to the break as I hadn't had any time off in over five months since Christmas.

When early May came I realised that I had never received a response back to my holiday request in February but as no response had been sent I presumed everything was in order. My thinking was if there was an issue surely this would have been brought to my attention in the first week the original email request was sent. Sure this was basic management and looking after the teams well being was important.

Holiday requests in any team should be dealt with promptly as employees annual leave is their personal leave to be taken on holidays and other needs as they arise. Employees need to be able to take the holiday they want but if there is a genuine work issue or deadline that needs to be met and conflicts with a holiday request, then this should be brought to the employees attention immediately. In every job there are times when work commitments will take precedence over holidays, this is the norm and I appreciated that. But we all need holidays as otherwise work can feel like prison and having holidays dictated to you by your manager is not appropriate and bad management behaviour.

What was ahead of me was unthinkable but with my management team anything was possible. In mid May in the week before I was due to take my holiday I received a meeting request from my manager. It was for early Tuesday afternoon. Just before lunch on Tuesday she came over to me and asked was I ok for the meeting and if my team leader could attend. I said that was fine but once I knew my team leader and manager would be there I knew it was going to be a one sided meeting where once again I would be dictated too and the two against one bullying philosophy would take control again. I went out for lunch and prepared for the meeting ahead. It was clear it was going to be about my holiday request sent in three months previously and even though it hadn't been explicitly stated that this was the case, I wasn't stupid, I knew what was coming.

2.30pm came and the meeting started. I got the usual talk about how busy the team were and that the management team were working every hour god sent and that critical deadlines were coming up. Even though I knew the team was relatively busy, it wasn't as busy as what my manager stated and working crazy hours was a decision of choice not necessity. There was no need to work to midnight and at weekends, this was what they liked doing, but the concept of a work life balance had yet to dawn on them.

After five minutes of stating how busy the team were my manager got straight to business. She said I see you requested a holiday in late April. I said no it was early February. My manager then stated no you only requested it on the HR computer system in April. I said yes that is true because I only got access to that system in April but as you are aware the holiday was requested by e-mail in February. Having a meeting about this request three months later was unprofessional and not appropriate. Well I didn't actually state this but it is what I thought in my head. I knew now they were trying to catch me out at every given opportunity as they wanted to make sure they were in the right even though I knew this wasn't true. She stated I see you're doing an exam on Wednesday the 23rd May and you have applied for this day off and the Monday and Tuesday. I said yes I need those days as study days and want to use my annual leave for them. My manager stated this was a problem as we were busy with audits but that they had a discussion (team leader and manager) and that they would allow the leave on this occasion. I thought to myself,

I'm doing an exam, surely these days off cannot be an issue. Even if they weren't an issue the management wanted to make a point that they were in control of allocating holidays and that they had the power to approve or disapprove holidays.

This may be the case but annual leave days are the employees' days to take and I had to take annual leave days off to cater for studying as no study leave was forthcoming. I was only getting the minimum government approved holidays (in Ireland) of twenty days; the company was not giving me more. The upshot was that I had my first three days of the week off approved. At least this was something even if it had been a difficult and lengthy journey to get these days off.

However the Thursday and Friday of that week, days that I needed off as I was going on a short family break would be a different matter altogether. My manager stated categorically that these days were not going to be approved and that they conflicted with the workload of the team. I obviously was not happy as if these days off had been a problem they should have been brought to my attention in February when my initial holiday request went in. I remained calm and responded to my manager by stating that I had a holiday booked with my family and that I needed these days off. She again stated that work came first and that under no circumstance would this holiday be approved. I was angry now but I was keeping my emotions under wraps and keeping quiet. I said to my manager in a polite manner that I was taking these days off and that if it was a problem I should have been told earlier. I believed whether rightly or wrongly that I was entitled to this holiday. Normally I wouldn't be as forceful as this but months of bullying had eaten away at my confidence and I was determined not to lose this battle. Was an extra two days off really going to affect the team enormously? I doubt it. I firmly believed my manager wanted to reinforce her management technique and style by dictating that I work these two days. I am headstrong by nature but as a working professional I am always open to compromise. This didn't seem to be forthcoming from my manager. The meeting carried on for another five minutes when my manager asked me to leave. I had merely stated that I was taking the extra two days off. After all I had applied for these three months earlier. My team leader mentioned before I left the room that she thought I was argumentative. I had barely opened my mouth in the meeting, thinking that staying quiet was the best way to approach it. Obviously I defended by corner but when you have a situation like that and a company who promotes a two versus one policy in meetings, defending my corner was just a natural reaction. Thinking back they were trying to provoke me into a reaction where they could dismiss me in an instant. I luckily had the foresight to see this trap being set even if I did feel I needed to be defiant on the issue of the extra two days holidays.

When I walked out of the meeting room, I felt disgusted at how I had been treated again. I had done nothing wrong. I did everything by the book and yet again I was being portrayed as a difficult employee who was argumentative. There was no question my relationship with my manager had broken down but this episode was to me another form of bullying. My team leader and manager stayed in the meeting room for at least another 45 minutes after I left. They were plotting their next move. I went home that evening seething with anger and stressed. I knew my management team were never going to change but they might give me a break once in a while. Well it wasn't too much to ask but there was no chance in hell that was going to happen.

The following morning I went into work, with my head as clear as it could be. I opened my inbox and went through the vast array of e-mails, but one stood out. It was from my manager. My team leader and the head of finance had been included on the e-mail. Had yesterday afternoons meeting just got serious?

The e-mail started by stating that this is a response to my holiday request submitted in late April on the HR holiday system. This was just a sly tactic as my manager knew as well as I did that the initial holiday request was submitted in February. Just another bullying tactic I thought. She said that she was approving two weeks leave I had requested for September. This was great; I had two weeks off in September that I didn't even want. I had only requested these days as I was told to request two weeks off as my manager wanted to know when everyone was going on their two week break. This was only provisional to me. Of course taking a holiday in August was off bounds as my manager would be on holidays then. My team leader didn't take holidays. She was a work-aholic and as far as I could see she didn't have much of a social life outside work. My guess was that her holiday was working and if she didn't work, life would be too boring to cope. She was very nervous and from my vantage point, socially challenged. But when one lives like this they forget that the majority of people love their free time outside of work and have families and friends to see.

My holiday request for the Wednesday exam day was officially approved, only three months after the request was sent and then she formally approved the Monday and Tuesday annual leave days. However she stated that external auditors were coming in the following week and that these annual leave days were not suitable but that they would be granted to facilitate study. Wow, how generous I thought. My employers were approving my own annual leave days which I was going to use to study. And the fact that auditors were coming in the following week meant that I should be overly thankful for the days off. I still couldn't understand how auditors' coming in the following week affected days off the previous week.

However as I read more of the e-mail the bombshell hit. The Thursday and Friday after my exam were not being approved as they were not convenient in terms of meeting deadlines. To me this was a disgrace. I was being declined holidays because deadlines had to be met. Sure they have to be met in every job, this was part and parcel of working life, but this surely wasn't the real reason. The real reason was she was the boss and she was telling me that I have to work under her terms and that was it. All my work was up to date so implying deadlines had to be met was a weak argument.

If my week break had been an issue why wasn't it raised in the week after I requested them in February? I asked this question during the meeting the previous day but of course was told that she was too busy to look after holiday requests. So indirectly she was telling me that her teams annual leave requests and work life balance was not important and she couldn't care less. Was this her management policy or the policy of the company as a whole? Who knows but she was definitely let get away with treating her staff with contempt when she should be guiding and supporting them.

The email went on to say that my team leader had received an e-mail holiday request from me in February but that I was verbally told these would not be approved until they were inputted on the HR holiday system. This was madness, there was no reason for my manager not to approve my holiday in the three months from February to May, none at all. I couldn't recall ever my team leader stating that my holidays were not being approved because of something minor like this. This was just one more lame excuse and cover up on their side.

I was told it was not appropriate for me to book a holiday or in my case a short family break without holiday approval. Yes this would be understandable if I was booking a two week holiday but the holiday and annual leave system works two ways. A manager has to look at requests promptly and not leave it until three months later. The excuse I was given was that she was busy. We all are busy, such is life. But the soft skills of management are just as important as the hard ones. I was now being told I couldn't book holidays until my manager approved holiday requests three months later. In a normal working world this would never work. I said to my manager she should look at requests within one week of them being sent even though I think a two, maybe three day turnaround was realistic. She denied my request stating she worked on a monthly rota and only looked at requests at the start of every month. I stated my point of view saying this was not ideal as we all have families and need to know when we can take holidays. My manager didn't understand this, which was clear as day. During the meeting the previous afternoon when I mentioned that I had never had any problems taking days off in previous employment, this was thrown back in my face and my manager stated that I was working for a different company now and that they did things differently. They sure did, I was under no illusions about that now. I knew this company was stuck in the dark ages and my boss was living in a work culture that was obsolete and that destroyed employees' well-being who worked under her tenure.

When I said to my manager that we should be involved in meetings with external stakeholders and that our holiday requests should be taken into account when setting deadlines, I was told that this wasn't the way she did business. Well the way she did business was hardly professional and if she couldn't listen to colleagues on her team with respect, well what was the point of working in her team?

I had now read the e-mail in its entirety, but I needed time to reflect on it and respond in the correct and dignified manner. I rang my wife to let her know what was going on and she gave me good support and advice. I should respond, but to be firm and professional. It took an hour in the morning for me to think about an appropriate response. I didn't want to fuel the fire that had started to burn uncontrollably; I wanted to put it out. Therefore what I needed to say had to be polite but firm. I didn't want to lower my standard and send a provocative e-mail. Although one might argue I was well within my rights to do so as I had been putting up with the bullying tactics for nearly six months now. If I was less experienced and maybe a green employee just out of college I could easily have responded with expletives and let myself down badly. There was no denying the stress was getting to me but I was determined not let the bullies win and get my one weeks holidays. This was the least I deserved. The e-mail I replied with to my manager is below.

"The reason I applied for a week off in May was that I had an exam and wanted time off to prepare for that and then to take a family holiday to de-stress and unwind. I think everyone deserves a week off or break every five to six months and I haven't had a week off since December. Since I didn't hear anything back from my original holiday request in February I assumed it was ok and hence booked a

short break away that has been paid for. On this basis I would be grateful if you could revisit your decision and grant the holiday request."

I thought the reply was sincere, nicely written and to the point. I didn't want to go into too much detail regarding my manager's previous e-mail as this was not in my opinion the right way to approach it. There was no point in stooping so low to her level.

The question now was if the e-mail would work and get my manager to grant the holiday request. She would have to change her ways to do so as for her it wasn't in her nature to give up control and now she had a sidekick to back her up in the form of my team leader. To humour myself I gave them nicknames of dastardly and mutley from the old classic cartoon. I would have a chuckle when I used think of this. Any little thing to make me cope was good now.

After lunch I received another invitation to a meeting at 4.30pm that afternoon in the basement floor meeting room. It was like a dungeon and had no air inside it, more like a prison cell. The basement floor tended to smell a lot as the stench of rubbish from the canteen filled the air. Again it wasn't just my manager who attended the meeting; she was backed up by her trusty lieutenant, the team leader. You wouldn't see one without the other now. It just reinforced my belief of a two against one policy the management team had. It was there to wear individuals down and intimidate them, make them feel inferior.

The meeting started with my manager stating that they were now willing to give me the week off. I thought I would feel happy, relived, overjoyed, even something good, but ultimately I felt nothing. I was mentally drained now and couldn't care less whether they gave me the holidays or not. For them it was just a power trip, but my journey in the company was coming to end, whether I found another job or not, I had had enough. I knew there was a catch to giving me the week off, something had to give. They would give me something good with one hand and take it away with the other. My manager proceeded on a rant, a tirade of abuse. She said I was unprofessional, argumentative, lacked respect, wasn't a team player and worked in isolation. The verbal attack lasted a few minutes and her sidekick threw in a few words also to make her feel important. I remained quiet during the meeting, took the abuse on the chin and only responded by saying I disagreed totally with their opinion of me.

Was there anything wrong with my work, anything at all? No my work was fine, completed professionally everyday and always with the utmost care. In fact I think I deserved a medal of honour for getting my work done whilst the bullying went on. My relationship with numerous colleagues internally and external stakeholders was great, yet for whatever reason I had been chosen by my management team as an easy target for bullying. The fact two women were bullying me meant it was always tricky in how to deal with it. If it had been a man, I might have been tempted to take him outside and sort him out Al Pacino style, not that that would have been correct, but with women it was a different ball game totally. I felt I had no choice but to grin and bear it and just continuously take the abuse. My main gripe though was why nobody at a senior level could see what was going on. Why did the people who could see what was going on ignore it and in some cases condone and join in the behaviour of my management team. This was utterly appalling stuff in a twenty first century work environment.

The meeting finished up after ten minutes, it was short which was a blessing. I left the meeting more stressed and angry but it was 5pm and time to go home. Great some fresh air and time to think things through.

On the way to work the next morning I thought the whole saga was over. The manager had backed down a little and given me the week off. It was time to move on and maybe settle into the job if that was possible. Well just when you think things are finished and a decision made it flares up again. I opened my e-mails to find a ten line e-mail from my manager sent at 8pm the night before, outlining everything she had said in the meeting the previous afternoon. This was like getting punched just before I was about to hit the canvas. Surely the referee had rang the bell, I had definitely thrown in the white towel at this stage, so could she not give it a rest. I'm afraid not. I had gathered she was the boss but to keep ramming it down my throat was unnecessary. How on earth had she even became a manager, a blind man could see she had no managerial skills and no

139

interpersonal skills whatsoever. She was a walking HR case or in America a walking lawsuit. Excerpts from the e-mail she sent are below.

"I need you to work as part of the team and not in isolation. The attitude displayed must change as it cannot continue. If we experience argumentative behaviour or a lack of respect going forward, we will be treating it very seriously. In this instance we will grant the two days leave post your exam, however in the future leave must be approved before booking a holiday. The team leader discussed the fact that you had verbally been advised that leave needed to be approved in advance and that everyone has to have their leave approved on the HR system. In response to your question I confirmed that requests on HR system will be responded to on a timely basis. I also advised that leave requests are not approved until they are approved via the HR system".

All the above showed to me was that my manager was unbelievably controlling and she would not look out of place as a prison warden. A timely basis meant at least one month or more likely three months later you will get that holiday request sorted. I kept been told my attitude needed to improve yet I remained calm, dignified and professional throughout the whole ordeal. There was only one person, well two people whose attitudes stank, no prizes for guessing them. The e-mail had a forceful tone to it that was just uncalled for. Another excerpt from the e-mail is below

"We note that you do not feel that you have been argumentative and think that this is our opinion but that you have listened to the points discussed. We advised that your behaviour will have to change going forward and that you must be professional at all times. I advised that if past behaviour is repeated in the future, it will be taken very seriously".

Yes my behaviour was to disagree with their bullying antics and to stand up for myself. I admit that, but was that wrong? It was time to move on from this saga, the pain to get a week off of my own time was insane and not something I would not like to go through again. It was a stressful time, a time I should have been concentrating on preparing for an exam. When five o'clock came on the Friday afternoon before my week off I rushed out the office door, quicker than Usain Bolt. I was still being hounded up until the last second but I was relieved I had the week off. I knew it would go quick but it was time off I well deserved.

I had applied for a couple of jobs the previous week and I got a few e-mails and phone calls regarding these applications the following week. I decided I would do a few interviews and see what would happen. I knew I had to get out of my current job, bullying wasn't good for anyone's health and it was certainly time to move on. I'm always confident going into interviews, the worst thing that can happen is that they say no. After a couple interviews in the space of a week I was offered a new job. The terms seemed decent on offer, better than the current job so it was a no brainer for me. It was time to move on and put this chapter of my professional career behind me.

I was back in work when I received the phone call offering me the new job. It was late Thursday afternoon and I was beginning to wonder if that phone call was ever going to come, but luckily it did. There was a mixture of emotions getting that phone call, but relief was the main feeling. At the end of the day work is work, you still have to get up every day and commute and perform your daily tasks, but at least my journey to hell was coming to an end and a new dawn wasn't far away.

When I walked into work the following day I knew it was the day I had been waiting for, for at least five months. It was the day I handed in my notice and started a fresh. When I told my manager she barely said anything, just demanded I did four weeks' notice, which I agreed to do. I would have preferred to have left quicker but I could handle four weeks. After lunch my team leader came up to me and asked could she have a private word. I said ok but to be honest I wasn't interested in anything she had to say now. She could have said nothing but asked whether she was the reason I was leaving. The answer was clearly yes, definitely so, (well at least 50% of the reason) but I decided to keep the peace and declared the reason I was leaving was that the job was too administration based.

It was a white lie but I knew and she knew the reason I was leaving. She had just virtually indirectly admitted she was at fault.

Herself and the manager were bullies and got a kick out of it. She stated that she hoped I would leave on good terms with her, but it had gone too far for that. The reason I was leaving was predominantly the bullying from my manager and team leader and secondly the job itself. I had been promised an accounting job but all I did was mundane administration tasks a transition student wouldn't be happy doing. That had been further punishment.

My notice period would be interesting, how would they treat me now I was leaving? Would things escalate and get worse or would they give in and leave me be? The administration tasks got worse and any job without value I was asked to do. I think they were testing me hoping I would respond in a negative way but I knew the game they were playing. It was childish and I was too mature and professional to overreact. I just kept the head down and got on with it. The extra administration tasks were soul destroying, but it only left me in no doubt as to the nature of the individuals I was dealing with. They were pathetic, spiteful and horrible people with little or no compelling values at all.

The notice period dragged on a little but before I knew it, it was time to leave. The day before I left a few colleagues brought me out for lunch which was a nice touch. They knew what I had gone through and wanted to wish me well in my future. These people had to some degree became friends and at the very least they had been supportive throughout my bullying ordeal.

On the day I was leaving my manager asked us all in the team to gather in the canteen at 4pm for a presentation. I thought they might buy me something small or give me a bottle of wine. Well a token of thanks at least for putting up with the bullying would be nice. But no I got an empty card signed by half the team. She hadn't even gone to the trouble of making sure all the team members signed it. It showed the contempt she held for me yet I never did anything wrong. I had grown to hate my manager and team leader; months of bullying had taken their toll so to be moving on was a godsend. A few cakes were organised in the canteen but it was more a show for my manager's benefit. She wanted to save face and show that she had heart and was wishing me well in my new job. I didn't buy it, I just wanted to leave and keep running now. A leopard doesn't change its spots. I was thinking, who will she bully next?

Three days before I had left my manager had called the team into the meeting room as she wanted to make an announcement. There had been rumours she was moving on and I suspected this was just confirmation of that. My thoughts had been correct and she said that she would be starting in another reporting team in the same building the following month. This time she would be reporting to the head of reporting but that nobody would report into her. I wasn't surprised she was moving on, as it was widely known she was the primary reason why the accounting team was haemorrhaging staff for over three years.

Her departure had came too late for me and if I was being honest it wouldn't have stopped me leaving as my mind was made up on that score. Maybe the powers that be had realised my manager was a walking liability and costing the company staff, experience and ultimately money. Although it was never confirmed my guess was that she was deliberately being moved out of the accounting team and into another. It was plainly obvious she couldn't manage staff and colleagues below her so now it was time to see how she would fair reporting into someone above her. Only time would tell but I suspect she would struggle to settle into her new role. She was completely institutionalised so if she had been made redundant she would have found it very difficult to find another employer who would tolerate her working style. An internal move was her only option, but the damage she had caused wasn't reversible. The company wasn't going to try and get the staff back they had lost due to her. No this would be admitting there was something wrong to begin with and possibly indirectly confirming she was the problem.

What do you do if you are being bullied?

My story of bullying is not unique and cases like mine are all too common in the workplace. Maybe my case of bullying is in the medium range and I'm sure there are worse incidents occurring in companies as I write this book. The question is how do you deal with bullying and how can companies stop it and ultimately prevent it happening in the first place? There are many issues to think about in bullying cases. Namely what role do HR departments have in mediating and punishing the bully? Would an independent HR department mean that bullying cases are solved quickly and tempt the employees who are being bullied to come forward and report it quicker? Should companies and recruitment agencies delve deeper into potential candidates' professional history and see if bullying was an issue? Companies seem to be indifferent in their handling of bullying, lacking in ideas, wiping it under the carpet and hoping it disappears on its own. Admitting it happens is a huge issue for companies, as doing this admits there is a problem that needs to be solved. No company wants to get a reputation for institutionalised bullying.

The question is if your being bullied what is the best plan of action. As mentioned above you have to consider the consequences of any decision you take. Bring your case to the HR department and you run the risk of not being believed and possibly being sacked. It's you against the company. In every company there should be disciplinary procedures in place to deal with bullying and there should be a health and safety manual that incorporates a bullying policy. This manual should contain who you should go to if you have a grievance to bear. Some companies advise confronting the bully first and asking them to stop their offensive and belittling behaviour. This is not something I recommend and should be done with extreme care and caution. If you go down this road you let your bully know you now have a problem and give them time to form a defence of their own. The first person to talk to should be your direct team leader, manager or head of department. Or if this isn't appropriate as in my story then go straight to the HR department or a designated person who is independent in the company that will listen to your plight. But then to make things difficult not all and in fact most companies don't have a person you could describe as being independent.

Once a formal complaint has been made the company should record this in writing and then ask the perpetrator to respond to the allegations. The company will prefer to settle any dispute like this informally and ask a mediator to resolve any differences. If the case of bullying is too serious and has gone beyond mediation then formal procedures are the only means possible to get your case heard. The company should conduct a formal investigation into the allegations and come to a decision in a reasonable timeframe. While this investigation is going on, the victim and perpetrator should be separated in their work duties and kept apart as far is deemed possible. If a decision comes in favour of the victim the bully should be punished accordingly depending on the severity of the bullying in question. Demotion, written warnings, salary reduction or sacking are all possible punishments. Post decision action needs to be taken and implemented to stop the bullying reoccurring even if the bully has been sacked. Preventative measures are important.

If the decision goes in favour of the bully or if reporting it internally first is a not an option, then you can take the drastic action of contacting an employment law agency and they will explain your rights. This may involve paying a solicitor a fee for their service but it will make things formal and ultimately make you feel better. The employment law firm will advise you on the course of action to take, which could involve for example asking for all the information the company has on file regarding yourself. This can be done under the Freedom of Information Act 2003 in Ireland, The Freedom of Information Act 2000 in the UK, and in Ireland a company has 40 days to send out the information requested. Other countries have similar acts and by doing some basic research you will soon know your rights that pertain to your situation locally. Citizens Information bureaus, advice centres and various legal websites are always good at pointing you in the right direction regarding knowing your rights.

If you have to go down the employment law route then invariably you are going to want to make a formal written complaint to the company concerned. This is when things get serious and the company could get defensive or decide that they will settle the dispute amicably for both parties as any bad publicity concerned with bullying is not good for any institution, whether this is internal or external. It can be a long process but if you are determined it is one worth pursuing.

If bullying has taken its toll on your health, the fact is you might be out of work due to stress or heightened anxiety. A quick visit to your

GP will help here and stress can be diagnosed quickly. Depending on the seriousness of the bullying a prolonged absence from work might be needed anything from two weeks to six months. There is no set period, each case is objectively assessed and a GP will advise how much sick leave is necessary, in order for your immediate health to improve and stabilise. Office bullying can slowly grind you into the ground but there is hope. Never let the bully win and always stand up and be counted.

Survey on workplace bullying and stress

In the summer of 2014 I drafted up a survey consisting of ten questions. The themes of the survey were Workplace Bullying, Stress, Pensions and Social Media in Business. These themes were deliberately chosen to align with the three chapters in my book that discuss these topics. The survey was sent out to all my LinkedIn connections at the time, approximately 600.

My connections had a broad age range from 18 to 70 and nearly all had lengthy professional experience in varying companies and roles. This meant the majority of respondents were diverse in regard to age profile, sex, levels of experience and companies worked for. I believe the survey is reflective of real life scenarios and an accurate indicator of results if scaled up to a larger and broader audience. When the survey was closed in March 2015, 250 people had responded. The results of questions one to five are discussed below with the others questions discussed in chapters four and five.

Q1 Have you ever been bullied in any company you worked for?

Answered: 250 Skipped: 0

YES
33.20% (83)

NO
66.80% (167)

This question asked whether the respondents had encountered bullying personally during work. The results are clear with one in three stating they had been bullied and two in three stating they had not. I envisaged a higher result coming back YES but for one in three out of 250 respondents to state they had been bullied surely is a worrying statistic. My opinion is that some individuals may be unaware they are being bullied or might dismiss probable bullying as part of their normal working life. If this was indeed the case then the results could have been more profound. Statistics like this show that companies need to be more focused in tackling workplace bullying. They cannot afford to potentially lose 33% of their staff due to the sickening behaviour of their colleagues and managers.

Some reasons noted why respondents thought they were the victim of
bullying

- They had a better education than their boss
- They were a graduate and seen has a threat to their bully
- They were new to the company where redundancies had just occurred. They felt they were not made welcome because of this
- They were treated badly if they didn't work long hours
- They were overworked and called names
- Ignored and ostracised by permanent staff when working as a contractor

Q2. If you answered YES to Q1 what type of bullying did you encounter?

Physical - aggressive or violent behaviour aimed towards you – 2.4%

Verbal - abusive, offensive or degrading language aimed at you – 16.8%

Non verbal - being ignored, or ostracized for no apparent or justifiable reason - 20.4%

Cyber - excessive email, Instant messaging, texting by colleagues that you deem unacceptable – 4.8%

Micro Management - your work being constantly checked and frowned upon on a continuous basis – 16.8%

Overworked - being given excessive work to do when it is abundantly clear you don't have the capacity to do it or have not received adequate training to do it – 15.6%

Intimidation/Confrontation - seniors implying that if work isn't done you won't gain a promotion, or be able to take annual leave as requested etc - 13.2%)

n/a - answered NO to Q1 - 64.8%

Total Respondents: 250

For this question I gave respondents the choice of seven options. Each option represented a theme of workplace bullying that an individual might realistically face in their day to day working lives.

From the above data, you can see that verbal, non-verbal; micro-management and being overworked are the most prevalent types of bullying experienced in the workplace by those respondents who answered YES to question one.

Q3 Have you ever left a job because you were being bullied?

Answered: 250   Skipped: 0

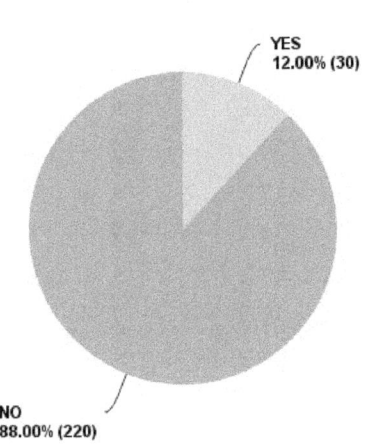

YES
12.00% (30)

NO
88.00% (220)

12% of all respondents say they have left a job because of bullying which seems quite low. However if you analyse this differently and match the 30 respondents who say they left a job because of bullying against the 83 who stated they had been bullied, then the result is far more alarming. Now the survey reveals 36% of those bullied left their job. That is slightly more than one in three, but staggering all the same. This reinforces the need for companies to take the threat of workplace bullying seriously and to curtail the damage it causes.

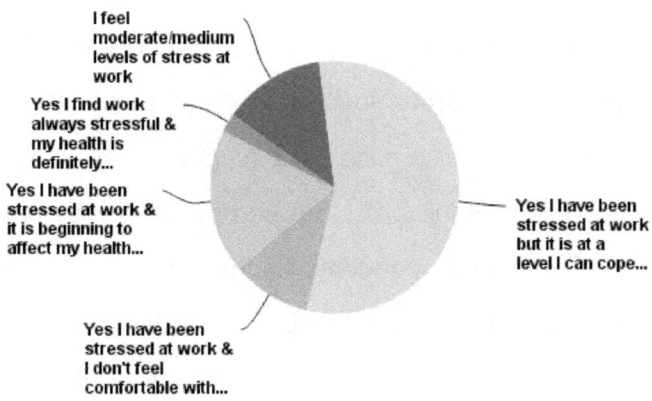

**Q4 Have you ever been stressed at work?
Please tick one box**

Answered: 250   Skipped: 0

Yes I have been stressed at work but it is at a level I can cope with
- 53.6% (134)

Yes I have been stressed at work & I don't feel comfortable with this

– 10.4% (26)

Yes I have been stressed at work & it is beginning to affect my health and work life balance – 18.4% (46)

Yes I find work always stressful & my health is definitely suffering 2.4% (6)

I feel moderate/medium levels of stress at work – 13.2% (33)

No I never feel stressed at work – 2% (5)

The above data shows that 245 out of 250 respondents say they have felt stressed at work, nearly 100%. Over half believe the stress they have suffered is manageable; with 21% believing the stress is affecting their health or beginning to affect their health. These results cannot be ignored. Whilst I cannot interpret how long the stress has gone on for from the survey it does reveal a worrying statistic, and that is stress cannot be avoided in the workplace. It could be argued that a certain level of stress is good for us; it keeps us focused on the task at hand and heightens our awareness to possible dangers surrounding us. But continuous stress is not good. If nearly 100% of the respondents have suffered stress than it is reasonable to infer that a certain percentage of these suffer unhealthy levels of stress on a regular basis. Stress can be a result of workplace bullying which in turn can be a further reason for individuals to leave their jobs. Respondents stated some of the reasons for suffering stress were, deadlines in work, financial issues, bullying, no work-life balance and being overworked.

Q5 **Have you ever rang in sick to work because you were suffering from stress?**

Answered: 250   Skipped: 0

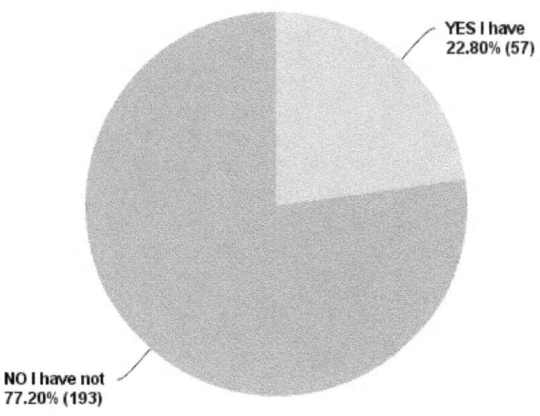

YES I have
22.80% (57)

NO I have not
77.20% (193)

The above question was asked to see the true cost of stress to individuals and companies in lost working days. Some respondents stated they rang in sick when they knew their employer did not pay for sick leave. That showed on one level that the stress suffered was acute. The results show nearly one in four said they rang in sick to work because of stress.

Whilst I can't attach a monetary value to the number of days lost to employers, it would be significant. If according to this survey a quarter of staff are ringing in sick because of stress either on an occasional or regular basis, surely the issue needs to given the importance and awareness it deserves. Businesses rely on staff to make them profits. If they are not turning up to work, nobody wins.

Chapter 4

Pensions –

A ticking time bomb!

Introduction

Since the financial crisis hit in 2007 a topical issue in media and television has been the effect the stock markets have had on company pension schemes, resulting in catastrophic losses for employees. Ignorance is bliss they say but not so when the lavish pension you dreamt off gets wiped out in a few short months. But even after the markets crumbled and pension pots evaporated into thin air, most pensioners still assumed they were protected and would be ok in retirement. It didn't affect them, did it? Unfortunately ignorance didn't save individuals pensions; it only compounded matters to the point where there was an air of disbelief and astonishment amongst them. In this chapter I try to simplify the often overly and unnecessarily complex world of pensions. I outline in simple terms the main types of pensions, the types of investments they hold, the dangers of mismanaged pensions and what the future might hold for them.

Types of pensions and pension membership – a simple explanation

Active members – these are members of pension schemes who are actively contributing to the pension scheme on a regular basis, i.e. monthly. These members could be part of a non-contributory scheme whereby the employer contributes only to the scheme on behalf of the members. These types of schemes are rare.

Deferred members – these are members who have left the scheme (normally because they have left employment with a particular company) or have stopped contributing to the scheme. At one time they would have contributed on a regular basis. The accumulated pension value can be transferred to another scheme or left to accrue further benefits until retirement age.

Pensioners – these are members of the scheme that are now being paid a pension from their accrued benefits. They would have previously been classed as active or deferred members depending on their individual situation but now have reached retirement age and can draw a pension.

Defined contribution schemes (DC) – in simple terms DC schemes are based on the amount of money you invest and what the market returns. Most people have bank accounts. The money you have in your account is yours plus any interest you earn minus any charges the bank takes. DC pensions work in a similar way. You get out what you put in. That is the contributions you make, plus the investment return the financial markets give you minus any fees the pension provider charges.

Personal Retirement Savings Accounts (PRSAs) and personal pension plans are DC in nature. With DC pension schemes the risk of losses are firmly with the employee or individual concerned. This can work both ways, if market returns are good your pension pot will increase, if you are unfortunate and the markets are poor then your pot will decrease. So DC schemes deliver unguaranteed returns. Poor returns can happen during recessions as it did between 2007 and 2013 (returns in equity markets have improved in recent years) with your investment choice and diversity of investments a key driver of returns. Consider the following example.

You are twenty five years old and want to start paying into an occupational DC scheme that your company provides. The likelihood here is that the company will at least match your contribution to the pension but most employers pay more than that. You earn €40,000 and are willing to pay 5% of your salary into the pension. Your employer will match this.

This means you will contribute €2,000 and so will your employer, a total of €4,000 a year. We will assume that market gains each year are 4%. In reality market returns will change year on year, and during recessions markets tend to be down. If we compound this figure out over 40 years until you retire aged 65 and assuming you pay in to the scheme every month for the 40 years the following return will happen.

Year	Contribution	Total Compounded
1	€4,000	€4,160
2	€8,160	€8,486
3	€12,486	€12,986
38	€343,881	€357,637
39	€361,637	€376,102
40	€380,102	€395,306

When you come to retire your pension pot is €395,306. This amount whilst sounding high is devalued by the power of inflation over the 40 years. I have not factored in potential pay rises over the 40 years, and whether you increase the contribution rate. You could also be unable to pay every month due to possible unemployment, illness or other expenses taking precedence.

Pension laws are different in every jurisdiction. This means you can invest in varying products at retirement. A proportion of your pension pot may be available tax free. Currently in Ireland as of 2015 you would be allowed take 25% in a tax free lump payment and use the rest to buy a pension from a financial institution. This can be guaranteed or not guaranteed but a financial advisor in the country you live in will explain the choices you have. These choices can include buying an annuity or investing in an approved retirement fund.

Let's assume you decide not to take the tax free lump sum as allowed in Ireland and take the entire sum for your pension. If you go to the market depending on whether you are female or male (as life expectancy differs for the sexes) your annual pension will work out as follows. If you are 65 it will be assumed that if you are a man you will live for at least twenty years but most pension providers will base this higher, at a multiple of 24 or 25. For women it tends to be longer, so you can add at least another two years on.

Therefore the €395,306 will pay you €16,512 in a pension each year. But in and around €17,000 will be your pension figure. Depending again on where you are from the €17,000 could be supplemented by a state pension. In Ireland as of 2015 the state pension is circa €12,000. This would give you an annual pension of €29,000. This is very low compared to the salary you may be earning when you come to retire. The above example is simplistic and makes many assumptions that may not be realistic for most workers. But it gives a taste of how much investment is needed for potentially small returns. For more detailed pension product information in your country you need to contact a pension advisor, as the example above is for illustration purposes only and to show the need to start saving for a pension early in life.

Defined benefit schemes (DB) – the amount you receive from a DB scheme should be defined, it says it in the title. However this defined part is a calculation made by actuaries using numerous assumptions that may or may not happen in the lifetime of the pension. Public sector DB schemes are funded essentially by the taxpayer and employees. Private sector DB pensions are funded by the employer and employees. Both are funded by the return the schemes investments make.

DB schemes are similar to DC schemes but the one major difference with DB schemes is that your pension pot is guaranteed and based on a percentage of your salary. The way this is calculated is changing and primarily depends on which jurisdiction you reside in. In Ireland it was typically based on either a half or two-thirds of your final salary, but changes recently to the rules of DB pension schemes have meant that pensions can be based on average salary over your working life. So for example in most public sector pension schemes which historically tended to be DB, an employee ending on €60,000 and having 40 years service would get either €30,000 based on a half salary pension or €40,000 based on a two-thirds pension. This would reduce accordingly if the employee had only 35 years or 30 years service and so on. The main attractiveness of DB pension schemes was the guaranteed nature of them for employees. Pay a set amount each month say 5%, this would then be matched or bettered by the employer and your pension was secure. However recent events such as the financial market crash have began to show the true cost of providing DB pension schemes. These costs can over time lead to the closure of the pension scheme and in some extreme cases the fall of companies. Quite simply employers were not funding the majority of pensions schemes adequately and they were susceptible to the unpredictably of financial markets

When severe investment losses happen it is the employer who takes the hit not the employee. This has meant huge losses for pension schemes and employers and ultimately reduced benefits for members. Sometimes only 50% of benefits are paid out or available for transfer (the value calculated by scheme actuaries) as the money is no longer available in the pension fund.

Continued bad market conditions and poor investment decisions can erode the value of the pension scheme assets. Poor returns ultimately drive up the cost of running the pension scheme and once the pension goes into deficit (its assets are less than its liabilities), the risk of winding up (pension closing down) increases. It can also cease accruals, become frozen (stop taking contributions) or receive funding proposals from designated pension boards. This measure happens when the scheme is in serious trouble and investment is needed from the employer to avoid winding up. When this happens pensioners get a lot less then they thought they would originally get and the guaranteed nature of DB schemes becomes worthless.

In Ireland pensioners are looked after first when schemes wind up and assets are distributed out accordingly (this may change in the future). The active members (those currently contributing) of pension schemes can suffer even greater losses if they want to transfer out their pension value to another provider or company. Actuaries will calculate a transfer value based on current market forces and the cost to the scheme. The risk of loss here is high. These DB schemes have in part bankrupted the Irish State and small to medium employers have gone into liquidation as the burden of servicing pension schemes was too much to take on.

What pension funds invest in?

Whilst your employer or pension provider will normally be in charge of where the monies are invested, it is worth understanding the benefits and dangers of investment securities and strategies. If you invest in DC schemes and PRSAs you should have access to choose where to invest your contributions.

Investment strategies tend to be devised by your pension provider or employers and these can be aggressive or passive in nature. You can choose a high risk, medium risk or low risk plan or a mix of all three. But whatever strategy you decide to take most pension provider funds are top heavy with equity investments.

Derivatives

The riskiest products in the markets are derivatives. These are based on market returns and the probability of certain events happening or not happening. Derivatives can include contract for differences, swaps, options and futures but are not limited to these. Their complexity is what gets them in trouble but for the risk taker this is the appeal. At the beginning of the economic melt-down in 2008, Lehman Brothers in America collapsed due primarily but not exclusively to overtrading in derivatives. Credit default swaps which are highly volatile and risky financial instruments caused Lehman Brothers in part to go bankrupt. The word *"securitisation"* became popular but unfortunately all for the wrong reasons. In simple terms companies were pooling various loans together (mortgages, credit card, car loans etc) and selling these as consolidated securities to investors. Securities backed by mortgages were called mortgage backed securities whilst the others were called asset backed securities. When the property market crash happened, people lost their jobs and could not pay their mortgages. Companies who had used securitization as an investment strategy found themselves in deep trouble with their returns and cash flow dwindling quickly. Once the banks creditors came calling, the banks were doomed. They hadn't the money to repay them. Other banks were just as naive as Lehman's but were lucky or some might say unlucky to get bailed out by their respective governments. It wasn't just banks that went belly up, countries did too like Greece. Ireland, Portugal, Italy and Spain were not too far behind. So choose a poor investment strategy and your money may end up gone forever.

Equities

Equities are shares or stocks in a company. You can buy or sell units at an agreed price based on the current stock market that those particular shares are trading on. They are classed as high risk predominantly because they are highly sensitive to changes in economic conditions, world events, natural disasters or any financial catastrophe that is deemed to impact the companies trading on the stock market. Recent armed conflicts in the Ukraine and the Middle East, projected profit or losses by companies, earthquakes, or typhoons that hit Japan recently, all can have a devastating effect on equity markets. The most well known collapse in the financial markets happened in Wall Street in 1929 and recently in the economic meltdown of 2007 – 2012. Whilst the reasons for these market collapses were complex and driven by many concurrent factors, the over reliance by investors on equities to provide gains, meant the value of companies stocks evaporated and in tandem pension fund values decreased substantially.

The simple truth is that no matter what financial advisors say or do the markets are cruel and don't discriminate. They will punish anyone who invests in equities. On the flip side the gains can be substantial and as I write this book the markets are recovering well especially the US and Irish market, whereas the UK and European market are showing modest growth.

Bonds

Bonds are classed as a low to medium risk. There are many types of bonds but in simple terms they are forms of loan agreements between one party (buyer) and another (seller). At the maturity date it is agreed that the buyer will repay the seller the principal amount and the interest amount agreed at the inception. The terms and conditions of deals differ as do the types of bonds bought and sold. For pension funds, government bonds (also known as sovereign bonds or GILTs) are the most common types invested in. Government bonds work off the same principal as outlined above and a country normally agrees to pay back interest on the bonds over fixed period instalments. A country's ability to purchase bonds in the market depends on their credit worthiness, financial reputation and whether they will possibly default on the agreement.

Cash

This is the simplest form of investment and the most liquid. In times of recession when banks need cash holdings the interest rate offered will tend to be higher and can reach four to five percent for some savings products. However in times of deflation or flat/low inflation banks will tend to offer lower interest rates. The ECB (European Central Bank) currently is enforcing a policy of zero to negative interest rates. This is because economic growth and consumer spending in the main EU countries like Germany and France is stagnant and banks don't want people saving money, they want them spending it or taking out loans. A more extreme policy that has been introduced in 2015 is quantitative easing which in simple terms is when the ECB starts printing more money. The prime reason is for countries to purchase government bonds off each other. Whether the real economy benefits from such an economic policy is open to debate.

Over a long period of thirty to forty years cash returns should be positive at around one to two per cent. Inflation will erode any gains.

Property

The old adage states that a property is worth what someone is willing to pay for it. In times of growing inflation and economic stability property prices tend to rise. The difference between what one owes for the property and its current worth is called equity or negative equity. Having equity build up on a property is good for investors.

Pension funds invest in property and the unrealised equity gain is one way how property funds make money. The funds can buy and sell and accumulate wealth accordingly. Rent on property also offers a steady income flow. However as the world found out in the recent economic crash, overvalued properties have left individuals overburdened with negative equity and unaffordable mortgages. For pension funds and investors the property funds suffered enormously with values decimated. For these reasons property is a high risk investment. Gains can be large in property bubbles and strong economic conditions, but the reverse scenario can mean the values of property portfolios are wiped out. Individuals may have to deal with crippling negative equity on their homes. When property prices rebound and values start increasing repossessions could dramatically rise as this is when the financial institutions who lent the money tend to be most ruthless.

Problems with pensions

Bad investments can devastate pension funds in the public and private sectors

As mentioned previously derivatives and equities can be a disaster for pension funds. This has been shown to be true recently in many companies' pension schemes. There are many causes and reasons why pension schemes give low returns. Bad investment choices, bad management and poor governance are the primary reasons. Whilst the financial markets are uncontrollable as to what they will return investment decisions are wholly controllable. This is the responsibly of the investment managers both internally and externally on pension funds.

Two of the biggest banks in Ireland, Bank of Ireland and Allied Irish Bank (AIB) suffered phenomenal losses to their respective pension schemes during the financial crash. Bank of Irelands cash deficit was well over €1 billion after the crash. It recovered to circa €1.1 billion in 2012 and €840 million in 2013. The recovery is being driven by the financial markets, the same markets that wiped out the pension fund to begin with. As the old adage goes the markets gives it to you with one hand, but takes it away with the other. Other large organisations with crippling deficits are Diageo (makers of Guinness) and Smurfit Kappa. Prudent investment management and some luck will hold the key to their recovery.

The problem here is, are we learning from our past failures and mistakes? A leopard doesn't change its spots right and repeated mistakes can easily be made. A friend of mine would say to me the reason why the Irish Rugby team kept getting beaten in France every two years (in the Six Nations Rugby Championship) was that they played exactly the same way every time, yet hoped the outcome would be different. In 2014 Ireland beat France for only the second time in forty years in Paris. The prime reasons being a change of management, coaching and philosophy. New ideas bring new results.

However the over indulgence of Irish investment managers in equities does not seem to be waning. In fact it may be getting worse. Equities caused huge heartache for the pension industry over the last ten years but statistics are telling us that this hasn't changed. A recent report from LCP Ireland (a pensions consultancy and research company) noted that Irish pension schemes were investing 50% of their portfolio of assets in equities compared with the FTSE 100 company average of 33%. Irish pension schemes deficits on the whole were getting larger even though the stock markets were up roughly 12% year on year from 2013 to 2014. Ryanair a well known airline carrier had a 77% investment in equities in 2013. This by any pension standards was worrying. Ryanair by nature are risk takers, that in essence is how they have succeeded, but being overly reliant on equities to generate high returns can be too risky as past experience has told us.

Pension levies and taxes

In Ireland the pension levy which is due to finish at the end of 2015 was and is a huge disincentive for individuals saving for a pension. Further to that it didn't help financial advisors or organisations who were trying to sell pension products to prospective clients. The reasons for the introduction of the pension levy are simple; the Irish government wanted an easy fix to generate more taxes. The pension industry was seen as a prime target. To offset the pension levy in the private sector the government stated they were reducing the rate of VAT (valued added tax) and that the money raised would be used to fund a jobs investment package, but this was of little comfort to an already stressed pensions market. The reality was the money would be used to service the country's crippling debt.

The private sector levy was initially a short term measure but since 2011 when it was first introduced it has raised circa €2.3 billion for the Irish government. Although I thought this tax would continue into the foreseeable future the government has decided to phase it out with 2015 being the final year of the levy at a reduced rate of 0.15% of the value of a pension fund, down from 0.75% in 2014 and 0.6% since 2011.

The public sector levy which was introduced amongst great anger and resistance averages out at 7.5% per employee which is high. Rumours in the Irish media have stated that this levy will be reduced or abolished before the next general election in Ireland in 2016. I doubt this will happen as it is too much of a cash-cow for the Irish government.

The pension levy was a bad idea; there is no doubt about that. Instead of introducing levies which lack any real foresight or planning, the Irish government and governments in general should look at the future big picture. In Ireland an ageing population and fewer people of working age will be the real issue facing the Irish government down the road. How will they fund these people in retirement?

Big fees

Pension providers charge big fees and with pension schemes there are administration and actuary fees for employers to factor in. Actuaries charge huge fees every month for reviewing schemes and carrying out valuations. My pension provider for example charges me 5% for administrating my pension, and although this will go down slightly the more I put in, it is still a huge expense and means saving for pensions is still unattractive. Many small and medium sized businesses have folded in the last five years and a big factor has been the cost of servicing pension schemes. Companies can no longer afford to provide these schemes and have wound them up and transferred the money into personal retirement bonds, PRSAs and other pension products for the employees concerned.

So why are pensions unattractive?

Let's take a basic example of a thirty year old married man who works for a company who provide no pension, but has access to a private personal pension like a PRSA. The man earns €50,000 a year which in today's economy is a decent wage. If you factor in the cost of living, mortgages, childcare costs, day to day expenses, car costs etc his net wage is soon evaporated. He works out that he has €250 to invest in a PRSA each month. This is €3,000 a year of which he will receive 40% back in tax relief (Ireland) as it currently stands in 2015. Most pension providers state they try to increase pensions by 3 to 5% each year. Let's take a more realistic figure and say in today's market 3% would be good. This figure will compound each year and could decrease if markets declined. I'm going to take a positive outlook, if maybe a little unrealistic and assume a 3% increase every year for 35 years until the man retires at 65. This means at the end of year one the pension scheme is worth €3,090. Year 2 a further €3,000 is invested bringing the total to €6,090, increased by 3% = €6,273. (I am using an annual compound interest rate and not a monthly one, so the total figure after 35 years is an estimate but a close one). After 20 years the pension pot is €77,600 and after 35 years is circa €178,000. This is a big sum of money but when it comes to pension pots it's quite small. Why you may ask, well here is the reason why.

As it currently stands in Ireland you should be able to take 25% of your pension pot as a tax free lump sum up to the value of €200,000. This can change if a lump sum has already been taken as part of a redundancy package during your working life. For the purposes of this example this is considered to not have happened. After the €200,000 (€800,000 pension pot) is taken the remainder is taxed at the standard rate up to €575,000 and the marginal rate thereafter.

25% of €178,000 above would be €44,500, leaving €133,500 in the pension pot. If this is a DB plan the actuary will calculate the pension on offer. It is likely to be on average €133,500 divided by 25 or even higher. The reason as touched upon earlier is that the life expectancy of men and women is increasing and pension providers will assume that pensioners will live until 85 or even 90 years of age.

The same applies for DC type schemes and when these factors are considered the pension on offer will be very low. The state pension will increase it further. It currently stands in 2015 at €230 a week or nearly €12,000 a year (in Ireland). This means that private sector workers on the main will be facing into having very modest pensions when they reach retirement age. What is likely is that something will be needed to supplement this income, but working in the twilight of your life might not be realistic. The only way to combat this is to start saving for a pension as early as possible and hope the compounding nature of growth will help the value increase.

Can we afford to invest in pensions when the cost of living is so high?

Pensions are a ticking time bomb. For most people it leaves them in a quandary, they think, I need a pension but I can't afford one at the minute. In Ireland roughly 50% of people working have pensions, that is they pay into an organisational pension scheme through their employers or have DC PRSA type pension arrangements whereby a pension provider invests money for an individual who pays monthly premiums. The majority of individuals though have small pension pots and these will only fund a limited lifestyle when they have to retire.

The question is how do we solve the pension time bomb and get people saving now when unemployment is relatively high and the cost of living for employed people is severe. Factor in mortgages, potential for increased interest rates, childcare costs and the average person today is struggling to keep their heads above water. Savings, what savings, sure how can people afford to do that. In 2012 it was reported in the media that in Ireland two out of three people have only €100 disposable income left each month when all bills and expenses are considered. In 2015 it's only marginally better.

How do you promote the value of pensions to anyone when over the last ten years pensions haven't made a penny when you average it out? Some years there have been gains, others catastrophic losses. From 2008 to 2010 losses were big in pension funds as the majority of organisational pension schemes had invested heavily in equities. Whilst the thinking behind equities is that they will increase your pension pot substantially over the long term, the exposure to short term losses is high. No more so in a deep recession. Governments have failed to see that the biggest barrier to entry as far as pension schemes are concerned is a lack of funds to invest. Short term costs are more important to the average worker. Worrying about funding a pension is not a reality for them. It is about the here and now for the average man and woman.

Our innate lack of knowledge

The lay mans knowledge of pension investments is poor. To be fair this may not be our faults. Pension products are unnecessarily complex and it is this complexity that bewilders individuals to the point where boredom and a lack of interest take over. When financial advisors try to sell you financial products they don't go deep enough into the risks involved. Maybe this is because no one would buy financial products if they knew the full story. Pension products are sold on the basis that they will increase by 3-5% every year without fail. This is just not possible. A sub note to most financial investments will say *"investments may rise and fall"* but one needs to be aware that *"fall"* could mean a big fall.

If you're a thirty year old man or woman starting a personal pension the potential to take on a higher risk product is there as you are a long way away from retirement. But at the same time do you want to be putting all your eggs in one basket and investing predominantly in equities. Probably not! By thirty five you might have 15-20k in your pension pot, not a huge amount of money but a start. If you had your money in an indexed equity fund or consensus fund for example in 2009, your plan value would have plummeted to maybe eight or nine thousand euro, maybe less. This is a huge hit and would be hard to recover in the short to medium term. This is the risk you take, so one needs to ask themselves am I risk adverse or a risk taker. But the reality for most people is that we don't have the time or interest to attain a deeper understanding of what we are investing in. This leaves us open to great heartache when we reach retirement age if our pension funds are decimated by poor market returns. My advice is always research as far as possible what you are investing in and the company or advisor you are letting take control of your pension.

It is only a business and a salary to them, but to you it's your livelihood and not to be taken lightly.

Public sector pensions can overburden the exchequer.

In 2013, the city of Detroit in Michigan, USA filed for bankruptcy with the primary reason being that it could not fund the DB style pensions it promised to its public sector workers. Other US cities may have to do the same, with Illinois state over burdened with heavy pension liabilities according to The Economist magazine in July 2013. As the employer takes the majority of the burden with DB schemes, it is the employer who will have to pay out the pensions no matter how bad the pension scheme does on the markets. In essence for the employee who may only contribute five or ten per cent of salary it means a guaranteed source of income when they retire. This is one of the primary reasons companies and even cities can become financially instable. The other main reasons are the investments. Equities and property have proved to be an unreliable way of generating positive returns though analysts will testify that equities do give favourable returns over the long term, thirty to forty years. This may be true to a certain degree, but the problem is these potential gains can be wiped out fast in turbulent economic times

Can we trust the pensions industry?

The simple answer to this is no. History especially the last ten years have shown the pensions industry to be inept at managing pensions and advising prudently. Even in 2015 some companies like Ryanair are overly exposed to equities, suggesting company's pension's advisors and managers have not learnt past lessons.

The Irish government's pension levy and lack of any real commitment to tackle the pension's time bomb that is ready to explode is very worrying for the Irish economy and pension savers. A suspicion that this levy may be extended or a new levy introduced down the road is a real fear, regardless of promises made to the contrary.

With an historic over reliance on DB schemes in the private and especially the public sector, the sustainability of many schemes is in question. DB schemes are closing and any new offerings by companies are on a DC basis. This is where the onus is solely on the individual to save for their pension, relying on good market returns for growth. It is abundantly clear in 2015 that the investment needed by individuals is far below what they need if they want to retire comfortably. Again as stated previously other pressing financial needs are taking precedence over pensions for many individuals. With the concerns raised above and lack of any real answers by the pensions industry and government, it is not unrealistic to assume the average pension investor today is disillusioned with the state of the pensions industry in Ireland.

Pensions from hell

The fallout from losses in DB pension schemes has been felt worldwide, but here in Ireland the damage and losses incurred in some pension schemes was unthinkable for many. Companies such as Diageo, Bank of Ireland, Dublin Airport Authority and most notably Waterford Crystal were badly hit.

Laws differ in many countries regarding who is entitled to what when a pension scheme becomes insolvent or winds up. In Ireland, pension laws change almost annually and can be hard to keep up with. Up until recently pensioners pension value was 100% guaranteed. This changed recently with pensioners now in some cases only entitled to 90%. The government has been ultra cautious in its approach to pensions legislation change, but the need for serious and robust research into pensions policy in Ireland is well overdue. Active and deferred members faced reduced value pensions depending on the money left in the pension fund. However what happened with the Waterford Crystal pension scheme has changed the playing field considerably.

This DB pension scheme was wound up in 2009 when the scheme was declared insolvent. The pension benefits accrued for all 1,800 members were said to be worth only a fraction of what had been paid in, in most cases being totally wiped out. It was an unparalleled situation that the workers had been left in. The once flourishing company had disintegrated in front of their eyes and employees with forty years plus of service were left destitute. Because those already receiving pensions were protected under law and those not receiving pensions were not, a group of employees in 2010 backed by their respective trade union took a case against the then Minister for

Social Protection in Ireland. The case was subsequently referred to the European Court of Justice.

The European Court of Justice ruled that the Irish Government had an obligation to protect employees of Waterford Crystal and potentially other employees of Irish companies who have had their pension benefits wiped out. They were scathing of the Irish government's lack of protection for the workers pension funds and perceived unwillingness to help the employees to be financially stable in retirement. The court found that the Irish government was in serious breach of the EU insolvency directive, a piece of legislation that protects employees' rights in the event of employer insolvency. Article 8 of this directive stated that countries in the EU are obliged to protect the interests of employees and former employees with respect to the protection of their pension entitlements when an employer becomes insolvent. It ruled that Ireland had failed to adhere to this directive, which did not do Ireland's reputation any favours when it came to our perceived perception abroad has a friendly and nice place to work.

Up until late 2014 the former Waterford Crystal employees were still in limbo waiting for the Irish government to come back with a package that would be agreeable to them. The Irish government before the intervention of the European Court of Justice had hoped the employees would be happy with the state pension of €12,000 a year. The ECJ ruled that any offering had to be at least 49% of their benefits. Eventually in December 2014, the employees' courage and persistence paid off and a €178 million package offered by the Irish government was accepted. It had been a hard fight to regain most of the money that had been lost through no fault of their own. Whilst the package offered had varying complexities attached the main offering was that employees would receive €1,200 lump sum for every year of service and between 78 and 90% of their full benefits. The UK government had agreed to fund 90% of employees' benefits in the British part of the organisation, and although what the Irish government offered fell short of this, on the whole it seemed a good deal. The story of Waterford Crystals employees six year fight to regain their pension benefits may seem unique, but my educated guess is that stories like this will become a disturbing reality in the near future.

Demographics of a country

The demographics of Ireland at present mean that in the year 2040/50 a huge proportion of the population will be hitting or will be at retirement age. This will lead to a high cost burden on the state and also it will mean people working longer, even beyond seventy years of age. This won't be realistic for most people, as with old age comes poor health. The USA, UK and many countries around the globe face similar problems. Pensions reform has all of a sudden became a real and frightening prospect as some economies have come to realise that over generous pension pots especially in the public sector have begun slowly to bankrupt countries. The problem here for employers and countries is that a pension agreement is like a contract and is pretty much 99.99% guaranteed in law.

Recessions and downturns in the economy and a lack of people of a working age will have a detrimental effect on the ability of governments to use taxes to fund retirement payments. In Ireland the national pension reserve fund was set up to look after future pension payments for an aging population. This in hindsight was an ingenious idea, one of the few previous governments enacted. The problem though is whether the fund will be big enough. The suspicion is and research shows that it probably will not. It currently stands at circa €7 billion and was raided heavily by the Irish government to bail out national banks during the financial crisis. A funding gap will remain and with the workforce decimated by demographic forces, the Irish government's future purse strings will be stretched to breaking point. A scary thought for most people in the 25 - 40 age bracket who hope to retire at 60 or 65.

So what does the future hold for pensions?

The truth is the pensions industry is volatile and unpredictable. What has happened in the past ten years could and most likely will happen again. That is why the Irish government and governments alike, pensions industry and investment managers need to engage in urgent talks that will give a foresight and guidance as to what the pensions industry will become in the years ahead. The Irish government has blamed the pensions industry (providers and consultancies) and vice versa over the last few years of reneging on promises and not disclosing all the facts regarding certain issues. For the sake of the average worker and individuals living in Ireland a concise and intelligent strategy needs to be put in place soon to tackle an industry that has lost all trust amongst the public. It is my view that consultants and actuaries' are overpaid for the work they do. The question is, are we getting value for money in these professions? Surely for individuals to be paid such huge salaries, in excess of €150,000 in some cases, we need to receive an answer to the pensions time bomb that is staring us in the face, that is how do we get people paying into pensions that will provide them with a viable income in thirty years' time, when the demographics of Ireland will see a lot more pensioners than people of working age. That is the conundrum the pensions industry and government face. I would not be confident that it will be solved anytime soon. In Ireland there are lingering doubts about the sustainability of the current pension system. These doubts are well justified and the population needs to be aware that the pensions they think they will receive on retirement in twenty or thirty years may not be realistic.

I propose a few measures that could possibly help the current situation. I do not go into them with great depth as this is not the purpose of this chapter, but mere touch on them as to give you the reader some food for thought.

1. *Government strategy* – a detailed strategy as touched upon above needs to be developed by the government, pensions industry and possibly investment managers on how to get individuals saving into pensions over the next thirty years. As of 2015 little or nothing has been done to this effect.

2. *Possible solutions to solve pension's crisis* – the strategy proposed in point one could include some of the following;

Incentivise pensions – continue the strategy of tax rebates on pension contributions and don't change this policy. The government if it gets more individuals paying into pensions will get a large chunk of this rebate back when it starts taxing the pensioners' income when they retire. It will also obviously save the government money by having less individuals relying solely on the state pension. Once the pensions levy is fully abolished in 2015, the government must not renege on this promise or introduce another tax or levy.

Discrimination - As part of a plan to incentivise pensions the discriminatory practice of prioritising pensioners' monetary rights than those of active and deferred members needs to be overhauled. The possibility is most paying members into schemes are unaware that as it stands in Ireland if they are an active or deferred member their pensions are not guaranteed when companies wind up or become insolvent. Pensioners' rights take precedence and their pensions are secure. As mentioned earlier in the chapter this was previously 100%

secure, but changed slightly when new legislation was passed in late 2013 in Ireland. The main points are noted below.

Where the DB scheme is **insolvent** and the employer is **solvent**, the priority is as follows:

(1). Pensioners now no longer have full priority. Where their annual pension is:

> ➤ €12,000 (which is currently the state pension in Ireland) or less, 100% of the pension will be secured
> ➤ Between €12,000 and €60,000, 90% of the pension will be secured
> ➤ Anything in excess of €60,000, the greater of €54,000 and 80% of the pension will be secured. This essentially means a 20% loss for the pensioners.

(2). Next, 50% of the benefits (excluding post-retirement increases) of active and deferred members. This simply means half of the pensions of active and deferred members are protected.

But pensioners still take precedence. You could say that active and deferred members are second in line to the throne. Whilst this act improves active and deferred members' rights it still is discriminatory in nature and predominantly favours the pensioner.

(3). Any remaining funds must be used to secure the remaining benefits (excluding post-retirement increases) of pensioners in the first instance, followed by active and deferred members, followed by any remaining outstanding benefits, including post retirement increases, of all members.

Where the DB scheme is **insolvent** and the employer is **insolvent**, the priority is as follows:-

(1). Trustees to first secure 50% of pensioners' benefits (including post-retirement increases),

(2). Then, 50% of the benefits of active and deferred members (also including post-retirement benefits) to be secured.

(3). Then, funds must be allocated to "*top-up*" pensioner benefits to a maximum of €12,000 per annum (excluding post-retirement increases), and then to secure the remaining benefits (excluding post-retirement increases) of pensioners, active members and deferred members in that order. Any funds remaining must be put towards paying any remaining benefits, to include post-retirement benefits.

(4). In the event that a scheme does not have sufficient funds to secure 50% of the pensioner, active and deferred members' benefits (including post-retirement increases) and to top-up pensioner benefits to a maximum of €12,000, the Act provides that the State will, subject to certain criteria, provide the necessary funds to cover the shortfall.

The above information solely relates to Ireland and is readily available from many sources including government agencies, employment law practitioners, pension providers and your own financial advisor. All government websites will have information regarding to the pension laws that pertain in the state you live in. Citizen information websites can be useful too. In Ireland valuable information is available on www.citizensinformation.ie or www.pensionsauthority.ie.

The new legalisation above hasn't changed the playing field substantially as far as the legality and rights of members go. Pensioners still hold the primary rights when it comes to the distribution of assets in DB pension wind ups and insolvencies. The practice seems unfair and unethical. The reasoning may be that current active and deferred members have time on their side to accumulate a new pension pot. For members aged over fifty this is unrealistic and possibly unrealistic for most members. The case taken by the former Waterford Crystal members against the Irish state has meant that it is no longer an option for former employers and the state to wipe losses of pension funds under the carpet and claim a lack of responsibility. Pension members rights is a murky ambiguous area which needs to be restructured to give all members fair rights resulting in a level playing field.

Promote savings – it may seem simple put the government needs to promote savings again whether that is in the form of government savings schemes or higher interest rate on government savings products. Economic conditions have not helped in this area. If the Irish government continues its policy of direct taxation reduction as of 2015, then this will potentially increase individuals' disposable income. However indirect taxation continues to increase year on year offsetting any gain made from income tax reductions. If the government is serious about promoting increased pension savings their taxation policies need to incorporate this.

Advertising – as its stands the advertising of pension products by pension providers is limited. Recently there was a radio and billboard campaign by a well know pension product provider in Ireland that generated increased awareness of the pensions issue facing us as a country. The success of this campaign has yet to be confirmed. Unfortunately with increased advertisement the uptake of pensions will remain relatively low. Over 50% of private sector workers hold pensions of some form. In the long term this is not sustainable as far as the government is concerned. Therefore some investment now in educational advertising might help solve the situation if only in the short term.

Education – the complexity of pension products can bewilder people and leave them with a sense of apathy. Any organisation along with the Irish government need to have education has a core part of any strategy that is put in place to tackle the pension's issue. Promotional and educational leaflets should be sent to households. Organisations should engage in more frequent contact regarding pension products and investments to their employees. This is a necessity.

Governance - greater control of investment strategies needs to be put in place. The Irish government could consider introducing limits of investments in certain financial instruments, namely derivatives and equities once an individual reaches a particular age. This policy would be hard to enforce and would pose difficulties for investment managers, but it would mean that a pension fund is not wiped out during an economic crash. Keep it simple when an individual reaches 50, he should be given the option of reducing his equities and derivative holdings to between 40 and 50%. If the individual declines he should be explicitly told of the risk entailed.

The reduction or abolishment in use of asset backed securities, short selling and securitization would help pension funds to become more stable. The flip side is that they may not make as much money but the option is worth considering.

Reduce fees by pension providers – I currently hold a PRSA. The administrator of this product charge 5% on all contributions made, reducing as the value of the pension increases. Transfer values are not charged a fee. For every €200 invested €10 is lost on fees, it my seen small but over time it adds up. If a more open and better designed fee structure was developed it may encourage increased savings by clients.

Trustees – the trustees of schemes are primarily responsible for their management. It is up to them to monitor the monetary gains and losses in the schemes and maintain communication with the relevant stakeholders, the employers, employees, investment fund managers and unions where applicable. The management of pension schemes in the last ten years especially in Ireland has been appalling. DB schemes in particular have been poorly managed with high losses. Trustees need to be made accountable for these losses. It is essentially a white collar crime, as they have managed members' money to the point of obliteration. Stringent penalties whether these are fines, or lifetime bans from the pension industry need to be considered, enacted and enforced. In my opinion the current regulation in Ireland relating to this area is extremely light touch, bordering on non-existent.

Penalties - making pension providers and investment managers responsible for any losses incurred on the pension funds under their management is an option that needs to be seriously looked at. Poor advice and investment strategies were the controllable parts of what went wrong in the financial crash of 2007 to 2012. The financial markets may have imploded and this in itself may have been deemed uncontrollable but not having the expertise and foresight to see this coming was unthinkable. Letting institutions take no responsibility or having no accountability for their actions is an Irish phenomenon. White collar crime is not deemed as serious a crime in Ireland as it is in America for example. Enforcing harsh penalties for wreckless advice and bad investment strategies is a necessity to make sure advisors keep their eye on the ball. A mix of experience and education is always helpful here in preventing this happening in the first place.

Auto-enrolment or compulsory pensions – this idea is not new but it is something that needs to be seriously looked at. It would possibly be met with revolt by the public as it would be a draconian measure, but in my view it is urgently needed. Starting to save for a pension when you start full time employment at twenty two or twenty three years of age makes long term sense. Some companies don't provide pensions as they are deemed too expensive. When this is the case employers have to provide access and details of other pension products available such as PRSAs. Like taxes, a compulsory pension is something employees would get used to. Increasing the contributions as you get older would make sense and also a no obligation policy to contribute to a pension when unemployed. It may not be liked but it will help everyone in the long run. Ministers in Ireland have refused continuously to implement such as policy and the likelihood is this won't be introduced any time soon.

Pension reserve fund – Ireland has a unique fund called the pension reserve fund. It was set up with the foresight that there would be a deficit in the state pension coffers to fund individuals when they retired. The fund is now being used to fund an investment strategy program which is tasked with creating jobs. The reserve will probably also be used to support the public sector pension deficits. In my opinion this fund should be solely used to create a buffer zone for pension expectations in the future but inevitably this fund will unfortunately be used in a plundering fashion and assigned elsewhere.

Unemployment – continuing to reduce the unemployment figures will help the exchequer thus meaning monies can be given back to the workforce in future budgets. This extra money could potentially be used to save for pensions.

Language – the whole language of pensions needs to be overhauled. The needless complexities and unappealing presentation of data can turn the lay man off pension products. If you can't understand what you just invested in or paid money for then you have big problems.

Survey on pensions

The following survey asks two simple questions on pension membership and financial stability in retirement.

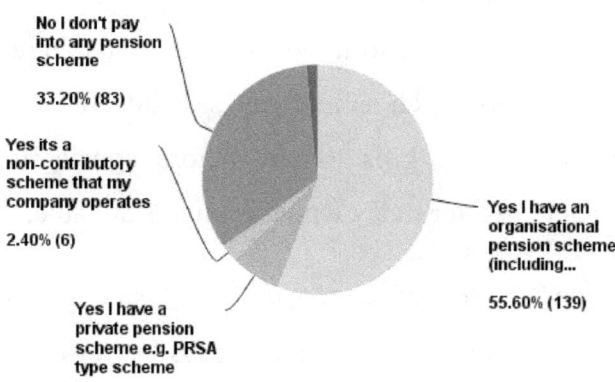

**Q6 Do you pay into a pension scheme?
Please tick one box**

Answered: 250   Skipped: 0

No I don't pay into any pension scheme

33.20% (83)

Yes its a non-contributory scheme that my company operates

2.40% (6)

Yes I have an organisational pension scheme (including...

55.60% (139)

Yes I have a private pension scheme e.g. PRSA type scheme

Answer Choices

Yes I have an organisational pension scheme
(including Additional voluntary contributions) - 55.6% (139)

Yes I have a private pension scheme e.g. PRSA type scheme - 7.2% (18)

Yes its a non-contributory scheme that my company operates 2.4% (6)

No I don't pay into any pension scheme – 33.2% (4)

Responses
Other (please specify) - 1.6% (5)

This question simply tried to gauge how many respondents currently paid into a pension scheme, whether company or privately operated. The results are better than I thought. Only a third of respondents stated they don't contribute to a pension scheme with nearly two-thirds stating they do contribute or are part of a non-contributory scheme. My understanding in Ireland is that a little over 50% of workers contribute to pension schemes. Obviously the current state of the Irish economy doesn't help matters. Unemployment is relatively high and the majority of workers have more pressing financial commitments such as mortgages, childcare fees, car costs, and grocery and utility bills to pay before considering pension payments. People live for today which is understandable.

The survey doesn't ascertain the level of payments by workers into the pension schemes and my educated guess is that the majority of workers are paying modest amounts each month. Basically what they can reasonably afford. But if I take the respondents answers at face value then the result is positive and shows potentially that individuals are realising the value of having a pension in place.

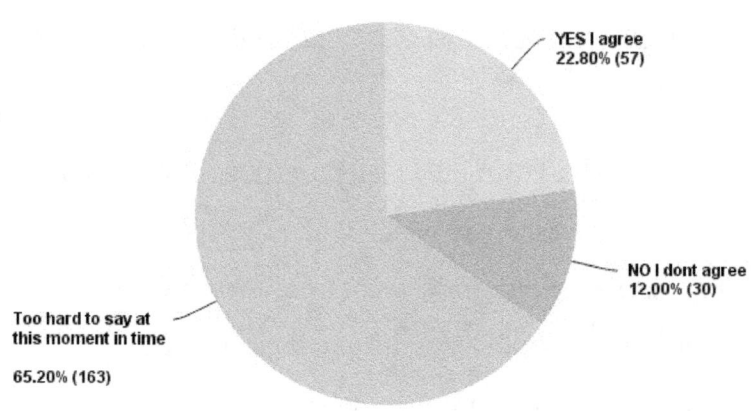

Q7 When I reach retirement I will be comfortable financially, i.e. I will have enough money to live on.

Answered: 250   Skipped: 0

YES I agree
22.80% (57)

NO I dont agree
12.00% (30)

Too hard to say at
this moment in time

65.20% (163)

This question followed on from Q6 by asking if the respondents thought they would be financially secure in retirement. Understandably a lot of respondents would be between twenty or thirty years away from retirement so trying to answer this question accurately would have been difficult. This is confirmed by 65% stating it was too hard to definitely say if they would be comfortable in retirement. Only 23% of respondents agreed they would be comfortable in retirement which is astonishing. This means the majority of 77% think they will either not be comfortable financially or are unsure of their financial situation come retirement age. This is worrying as the state pension in Ireland is only circa €12,000 a year which would be insufficient to fund the majority of pensioners' lifestyles. This may increase in the future but with the affects of

195

inflation any real increase will be modest. The result of this question can at best be described as negative with most respondents predicting financial uncertainty in retirement.

Some reasons why respondents thought they might not be financially secure in retirement

- Investing in a DB fund which they thought was unpredictable
- Had mortgages to pay which took priority
- Job instability prevented them from focusing on a pension
- Were paying small amounts into their pension
- They thought the future was uncertain regarding inflation and the economy in general
- They thought they could wait another ten years before starting to pay into a pension

Chapter 5

Social Media

in Business

So what is social media?

For most people social media is Facebook, Twitter and YouTube, the holy trinity you might say. But teenagers, twenty something's, thirty something's and even pensioners use different social media sites regularly so it would be naive to think usage is down to only three sites. In fact there are over 150 active social media sites out there, some are very well known, some less so.

Social media refers to the interactions and communication among people in which they create, share, and exchange information and ideas in virtual communities and networks, predominantly over the internet. Social media depends on mobile and web-based technologies to create highly interactive platforms through which individuals and communities can interact. Social media technologies take on many different forms including magazines, internet forums, weblogs, wikis, social networks, crowd-sourcing, podcasts, photographs, video, live-casting, gaming and social media blogging.

So is social media, a new phenomenon? Well in its current format - Yes. By that I mean internet, apps, smart phones, iPad etc. But the art of two way communication has been around for centuries, only now it has become digitised and global. Telephones, radio and television have evolved into emails, websites, smart phones and tablets. Anything is now possible. Humans are social creatures by nature; most of us like to talk and the vast array of technology platforms available make it easier than ever.

Social media is not just important for businesses, it's essential, but needs to be managed carefully. Remember an angry customer can tell twenty people, maybe more of her bad customer service, but if she gets on social media, she can tell the whole world.

A brief history of social media

1994 - Geocities was one of the first social media sites. The idea was for users to create their own websites, characterised by one of six "*cities*" that were known for certain characteristics.

1999 – Blogger is a blog publishing service that allows private or multi-user blogs with time-stamped entries. It was developed by Pyra Labs, which was bought by Google in 2003. Generally, the blogs are hosted by Google at a sub-domain of blogspot.com. As one of the earliest dedicated blog publishing tools it is credited for helping popularise the format. Users can share information, share photos and videos, add your location to posts via geo-tagging and use post time-stamping at publication, not at original creation. There is also a new preview dialog that shows posts in a width and font size approximating what is seen in the published view. It also included a new toolbar with Google aesthetics, faster loading time, and "*undo*" and "*redo*" buttons. In 2010, Blogger introduced new templates and redesigned its website. The new post editor was criticised for being less reliable than its predecessor. Another notable blogging site that followed Blogger was Wordpress. These two blogging sites would still be considered the most popular.

2002 - Friendster was a social networking website founded in 2002 which allowed members to contact other members, maintain those contacts, and share online content and media with such contacts. The website was also used for dating, discovering new events, bands, and hobbies. Users could share videos, photos, messages and comments with other members via their profile and their network. It was widely regarded as one of the original social networks.

2003 – MySpace website was founded in 2003 and built its audience by focusing on entertainment and music. MySpace was at its peak in terms of active users and profitability ($800m) in 2008 but went into steady decline after this point. At one stage MySpace's website was the most visited website in the U.S. The website's decline coincided with the ascent of Facebook and Twitter and a reason for this is attributed to the fact that MySpace used a *"portal strategy"* focusing primarily on music while Facebook and Twitter continually added new features to improve their social networking experience.

- Second Life is an online virtual world. A number of free client programs allow Second Life users to interact with each other through avatars. Residents can explore the world (known as the grid), meet other residents, socialise, participate in individual and group activities, and create virtual property and services with one another. Second Life is intended for people aged sixteen and over. Built into the software is a three-dimensional modelling tool based on simple geometric shapes that allows residents to build virtual objects. The Second Life terms of service provide that users retain copyright for any content they create, and the server and client provide simple digital rights management functions.

- LinkedIn is a social networking website for people in professional occupations. Founded in December 2002 and launched in May 2003, it is mainly used for professional networking. As of June 2013, LinkedIn reports more than 225 million acquired users in more than 200 countries and territories. The site is available in more than twenty different languages.

2004 – Facebook is an online social networking service. Potential users must be at least 13 years old to become registered users of the site. Users must register before being allowed to use the site, after which they may create a personal profile, add other users as friends, exchange messages, and receive automatic notifications when they update their profile. Additionally, users may join common-interest user groups, organised by their workplace, school or college, and categorize their friends into lists such as "*People From Work*" or "*Close Friends*". In 2008, Facebook surpassed MySpace as the most visited social media website in the U.S. According to USA Today as of September 2012, Facebook has over one billion active users of which 8.7% are fake. As of 2015 the site continues to grow in user numbers.

2005 – YouTube is a video sharing website on which users can upload, view and share videos. The website showcases user generated video content using Adobe Flash Video and 5HTML technology.

2006 - Twitter is an online social networking and micro-blogging service that enables its users to send and read text-based messages of up to 140 characters, known as "*tweets*". Tweets are publicly visible by default, but senders can restrict message delivery to just their followers. Users may subscribe to other users' tweets – this is known as following and subscribers are known as followers or tweeps (Twitter + peeps). Users also have the capability to block those who have followed them. Twitter allows users to update their profile via apps on their mobile phone and tablets. A recent study by Global Web Index found that usage was growing fastest amongst older people, especially with Twitter; confounding stereotypes that social networking is only for the young. The Sunday Times newspaper reported in September 2013 that Twitter was considering a public floatation worth $15 billion. Twitter began trading on the New York Stock Exchange in November 2013.

2010 - Pinterest is a pinboard style photo-sharing website that allows users to create and manage theme-based image collections such as events, interests, hobbies and art. In December 2011, the site became one of the top 10 largest social network services, according to Hitwise data, with 11 million total visits per week. In October 2012, Pinterest announced a new feature that would allow users to report others for negative and offensive activity or block other users if they do not want to view their content. Pinterest said they want to keep their community "*positive and respectful*". In 2012, it was reported that 83% of the global users were women according to www.engauge.com.

2011 - Google+ or Plus is a social networking and identity service owned and operated by Google Inc. It is the second-largest social networking site in the world, having surpassed Twitter in January 2013 according to Global Web Index. It has approximately 359 million active users. Whereas Facebook is the go-to service for connecting friends, Google Plus is more often used to meet strangers who share common interests. Google Plus acknowledged as much by adding its "*Communities*" section, which hosts a diverse mass of groups and lets users join a "*hangout*" - the popular group video service. "*An authoritative Google Plus account is one of the factors that will help you rank high on Google (search results)*" according to Business Insider and "*a popular Google Plus account was an important criterion in the search algorithm that ranks pages*".

2013 – Vine is a mobile app owned by Twitter that enables its users to create and post short video clips. Users must be at least seventeen years old to download it from the Apple App Store. The service was introduced with a maximum clip length of six seconds and can be shared or embedded on social networking services such as Twitter (which acquired the app in October 2012) and Facebook. Though Vine was initially available only for iOS devices, Twitter had been working on bringing the app to other platforms; Vine for Android was released on June 3, 2013 for devices with Android version 4.0 or higher. In a couple of months, Vine became the most used video-sharing application in the market, even with low adoption of the app. On April 9, 2013, Vine became the most-downloaded free app within the iOS App Store. Advertising agencies have been quick to seize on Vine's potential and it has also been used successfully in the field of journalism.

2015 – Facebook announces it is to introduce a money transfer platform. This will enable users to transfer money from their own bank accounts to another user's bank account. Whilst the service is in its infancy in social media it does show the potential social media companies have when it comes to entering the financial services arena and competing against players such as Western Union. Snapchat introduced a similar service called Snapcash in 2014.

Top 10 social media sites to use in business

Facebook

Founded in 2004 by Mark Zuckerberg, a college student in the USA, Facebook has risen to become the market leader in the social media arena. The initial idea was simple; a forum for students to interact and communicate on large college campuses in the USA, but this simple idea has become a global phenomenon. It offers hours of fun for its users and it is a must for the professional business user as it can be a great source of marketing and advertisement for any business. Initially aimed at the 18-35 age groups, Facebook has seen recently an increased usage in the 35-55 age groups. With the usage increasing, the potential it creates for business is huge. The film *'The Social Network'* starring Jesse Eisenberg documents how Facebook originated and became the global power it is now, a must see and great introduction to non-Facebook users.

Twitter

Twitter differs to all other social media platforms in that its concept is based on simple 140 character messages. These messages or *'tweets'* as they are commonly known can be obscure in nature to the mundane. Formed in 2006, many famous celebrities have Twitter accounts including Stephen Fry whose following keeps growing and growing. But for the normal business user, if used properly and if the right following can be attained, it can help give your business the advertising and marketing push it might need. This will take time and users need to be patient to get the most out of Twitter, but with user levels in excess of 500m people, it is well worth the time and investment. Twitters app and the increased usage of smart-phones and tablets have helped it grow in the last few years.

Recent mis-use though by certain individuals has led Twitter to tighten up its usage policy incorporating a reporting button for inappropriate and threatening tweets. After the England vs France Six Nations rugby match in March 2015, Nigel Owens the referee received numerous abusive tweets. This was not the first time this had happened to him and is a warning to the administrators of social media sites that zero tolerance needs to be shown to the perpetrators of such abuse. This is an area all social media providers will be keeping a close eye on over the coming years.

Google +

This is Google's proposed answer to the dominance Facebook has held in the social networking world since its inception. Google have dabbled before in social media platforms with Google Buzz and Friend Connect not reaching the heights needed to succeed. Orkut has done ok but it's primarily driven by Google Brazil and India. Google + is now recognised as the 2nd biggest player in the market, overtaking Twitter.

Unique features include Circles and Streams, that is the ability to place friends, colleagues, acquaintances and so on into different social groups, i.e. college, work, home friends etc. In the *"Stream"*, users see updates from those in their Circles. There is an input box which allows users to enter a post. Along with the text entry field there are icons to upload and share photos and videos. The Stream can be filtered to show only posts from specific Circles.

"Circles" enable users to organise people into groups for sharing across various Google products and services. Although other users may be able to view a list of people in a user's collection of Circles, they cannot view the names of those Circles. The privacy settings also allow users to hide the users in their Circles as well as who has

them in their Circle. Organisation is done through a drag-and-drop interface. This system replaces the typical '*friends*' list function used by sites such as Facebook.

Other major benefits include the "*Hangout*" facility, which is similar to Skype but free. Hangouts are places used to facilitate group video chat (with a maximum of ten people participating in a single Hangout at any point in time). Only Google+ users can join the Hangout if they happen to possess the unique URL of the Hangout. It's great for college students and especially businesses. Google + offers something different to Facebook and this is why it has crept up relatively unnoticed in user numbers, to now stand in excess of 500m users worldwide. Google have finally found the niche in social media they have been looking for and I think Google + will grow further in the coming years.

Pinterest

Pinterest is a web and mobile application company that offers a visual discovery, collection, sharing, and storage tool. Users create and share the collections of visual bookmarks (boards). Boards are created through a user selecting an item, page, website, etc. and pinning it to an existing or newly created board. Users save and share pins from multiple resources onto boards based on a plethora of criteria, e.g., similar characteristics, a theme, birthday parties, planning a vacation, writing a book, interior decorating, holidays and so on. Boards can develop projects, organize events, or save pictures and data together. Users can upload, save, sort, and manage images—known as pins—and other media content (e.g., videos and images) through collections known as pinboards. Pinterest acts as a personalized media platform. Users can browse the content of others on the main page. Users can then save individual pins to one of their own boards using the "*Pin It*" button, with Pinboards typically organized by a central topic or theme.

Users should be aware of certain terms and functions when using Pinterest. A "*board*" is where the user's pins are located. A "*pin*" is an image that has either been uploaded or linked from a website. Once users create boards and add pins, other users can now repin, meaning they can pin another user's image to their board as well. Pinterest has also added the option of making boards "*secret*" so that the user can pin to and view boards that only the user can see when logged into their own account.

The most popular categories on Pinterest are food and drink, DIY and crafts, women's apparel, home decor, and travel. The site can be used by professionals such as teachers and students to organise lessons and collaborate on projects. Businesses can create pages aimed at promoting their companies online. Pinterest now let's marketers access the data collected on its users. Pinterest Analytics is much like Google Analytics. It is a created service that generates comprehensive statistics on a specific website's traffic, commonly used by marketers. Retail companies use Pinterest for advertising and style trending. Data can reveal valuable relationships between consumer behaviours, products and content, where it can be collected and sold as marketing analysis. In May 2014, Pinterest was valued at $5 billion. It was the third largest social network in the United States in March 2012, behind Facebook and Twitter. Google+ has since dissected the leader board. Recent problems with scammers have caused concerns. Victims have been asked to fill in surveys purporting to be from actual companies, with free prizes on offer. They are then phished for their personal information and the promised free product is never delivered.

Instagram

Instagram was launched in October 2010 and bought by Facebook in April 2012. It is an online mobile photo-sharing, video-sharing and social networking service that enables its users to take pictures and videos, and share them on a variety of social networking platforms, such as Facebook, Tumblr and Flickr. Its photos are designed based on the old Polaroids and in a square shape. The video duration on Instagram is fifteen seconds compared to six seconds on Vine. In April 2012, it was announced that over 30 million accounts were set up on Instagram. The demographic most attracted to Instagram are those under the age of 35, with 90% of users in this age range.

Instagram is renowned now for trends such as Throwback Thursdays (TBT) and Selfies. TBT is a widely used trend on Instagram where users post pictures from the past with the hashtag #TBT. Famous celebrities such as Wayne and Coleen Rooney have embraced this trend. This trend usually includes pictures of users' early childhood, past special occasions, or monumental events. Selfie, a self-portrait photograph typically taken with a mobile phone or digital camera, has become a trending topic on Instagram becoming the *"word of the year"* by the Oxford Dictionary in November 2013. Recently the BBC discovered that users, mostly located in the US, were posting images of drugs they were selling and then completing transactions via instant messaging applications such as WhatsApp. The company acted quickly in response to the controversy stating that Instagram was not a platform to engage in such illicit activity and enacted new security to counter this.

YouTube

YouTube was founded in 2005 and proved such a success early on that Google decided to splash out north of $1billion to acquire it. So what makes YouTube so special? Well its main attraction is the vast array of content on the site. It is a video sharing site for all the public to use. Videos can be uploaded by any user or business. Links can be added to your website and videos can be embedded on to pages on your website, as if you had put it there yourself. Users have the ability to customise their personal channels with different designs to suit their preferences. Users also have the ability to earn revenue from their videos if they apply for the YouTube Partner program and a Google Ad Sense account. Users can leave comments under other user's videos and start discussions if they apply for a YouTube account. If you are looking to grow your business, YouTube is a free and easy-to-use service to share your brand in the public sphere.

Distinctions are made between registered and non registered users. Accounts need to be set up in order for you to be a registered member which gives you greater access to what might be deemed inappropriate or controversial material. Most of YouTube's revenue comes from advertising and in May 2013 they launched a subscription based TV channel service to compete directly with Netflix and other providers. YouTube's popularity has grown so much that politicians regularly use it to broadcast announcements and even the Queen uploaded her Christmas message once, but I guess she might have needed a little help to do that. YouTube continues to grow in 2015.

Yelp

Yelp, Inc. is a multinational corporation headquartered in San Francisco, California that operates an *"online urban guide"* and business review site. It was primarily funded by venture capital investments and began trading on the NYSE on March 2, 2012 at a share price of $15, valuing the company at $898 million. The $110 million raised in the company's stock offering allowed for further expansion in U.S. and international markets.

Yelp's service is based on the age old word of mouth premise and is community or local orientated in its strategy. Yelp's website encourages visitors to review and rate local businesses and services using a five point rating system The company's rating system and tools for filtering reviews have been the subject of both controversy and litigation. However this shouldn't deter companies from using Yelp, as better detection now exists on the site to find so called *"fake reviews"* by individuals to generate further business for some companies. The company's website provides a search tool by which visitors can access business reviews for companies that provide specific types of products and services in their area. The perception is that the majority of reviews are for restaurants but recent figures show this is around 35%, next is the shopping category, then beauty and fitness, entertainment and local services. The company's primary source of income is through business advertising on its Yelp website. As Stephanie Ichinose, Director of Communications in Yelp states *"it is all about connecting people with great local businesses"*.

Flickr

Flickr is a photo sharing site but a popular video hosting website as well. Acquired by Yahoo in 2005 for circa $35m it has grown to become one of the biggest social media sites around with approx 90m registered users worldwide. It is available to download in an app format for mobile users which is the most popular platform. One of the biggest groups on Flickr is something called *"Squared Circle"* and the premise of the group is simple, people take a photo of something circular and crop it into a square and upload to this group. Many businesses use Flickr to engage with their customers as they find that they are talking about their products and brands which can be helpful or sometimes not helpful to them. It's an easy way to have two way communications with your customer base.

A lot of art work is posted on Flickr and this can be a way to generate business for photographers and artists. Photos and videos can be accessed from Flickr without the need to register an account but an account must be made in order to upload content onto the website. Registering an account also allows users to create a profile page containing photos and videos that the user has uploaded and also grants the ability to add another Flickr user as a contact. Flickr also allows members to monetise their images. Flickr itself makes money from advertising and offers three types of accounts for members, free, adfree and doublr. These are based on storage capacity and adfree allows users to avoid ads for an annual fee.

LinkedIn

LinkedIn is a site that promotes professional workers who want to display their skill set to prospective employers and the public at large. As of 2 July 2013, Quantcast reports LinkedIn has 65.6 million monthly unique U.S. visitors and 178.4 million globally.

It is a forum to display your online CV (resume) where possible future or current employers can view your profile. You can list your work, education and life achievements on it. The idea is for professionals to become connected to other professional users within their business sector and beyond. You can request to get connected to someone, who in turn must approve your request for you to have full access to their profile. This is how you build connections.

There are premium packages available but the standard free package offers nearly everything the basic user wants. For companies there is the option to set up a page displaying your company details and it is a good place to promote your business to like minded professionals and others who could become clients in the future. A company e-mail is needed for this and a standard gmail account is no good. Other features of LinkedIn include group forums where discussions take place on various topics from marketing to IT. You can set up your own discussion group or request to join one you like. You can also advertise future events that are happening in relation to your business and update your profile with new achievements or positions. LinkedIn is now becoming very popular with the 18-35 age groups, but the main user base is still the experienced professional ranging in age from 30 to 50. It could in theory overtake traditional recruitment agencies to become a market leader in online recruitment. Only time will tell, but LinkedIn has put itself in a very good position to achieve this.

SlideShare

SlideShare as the name suggests is about sharing slides in a professional manner. This can be done by sharing presentations, online seminars, videos and various documents. Its popularity has been growing exponentially over the past few years and my view is it is an ideal forum to share business and educational information on various topics. Companies and schools can upload presentations that can be seen and used by employees and students alike. Other presentations can be uploaded that are merely there to entertain audiences or generate a reaction. Once the content is not illegal or deemed inappropriate it can be uploaded to the platform. This application is an invaluable tool in modern day social media.

SlideShare was launched in 2006 and attracted circa 60 million visitors every month. Its popularity led to a successful takeover by LinkedIn in 2012, with the amount paid just short of $120 million.

The benefits of social media

It can make you money – Mark Little was a journalist and news reporter who worked for Irish television for many years. He had a vision for a business that utilised social media and the vast array of content that it contains. His start-up called storyful.com simply discovers new material on social media whether this be on YouTube, Vine or Facebook, verifies the content to make sure its genuine, then acquires it and sells the rights to broadcast the material to news agencies across the world. The idea is simple but its execution is what has made this business succeed. Recently in 2014 the business was sold to Rupert Murdoch's Fox network in America for circa €18m. This business has shown anything is possible with social media.

A new media - As storyful.com has shown social media had become a new medium for sharing stories and content worldwide. Its real time effect has meant news and chat between friends is delivered in actual time. This is what makes it unique and gives it an unprecedented power. Traditional media platforms like radio, television and now internet have become more accustomed to embracing social media. Storyful.com now acts as an intermediary to verify content on social media meaning news agencies can be safe in the knowledge that the content used is factual and real.

Volume of users - Facebook has more than one billion users and Google+ over 500,000. With usage numbers like these the reach for companies' using social media as an advertising or marketing platform is huge. Unlike traditional media, utilising social media won't break the bank. What you as a company or individual spend is in entirely down to what you need. The majority of social media platforms are free. Extra services such as buying *"likes"* on Facebook, having premium accounts on LinkedIn or using analytical tools like Google Adwords to optimise your website power cost more. Most social media platforms offer a variety of add-ons to your account if you deem them necessary.

In essence what social media has done is make the world smaller, an extreme form of globalisation. Some social media sites like Twitter have seen a dip in numbers (primarily down to bad publicity over security and content), but on the whole usage across the board is growing rapidly. Therefore in the short to medium term at least social media is here to stay and should be utilised by individuals and companies in the appropriate manner.

Variety of sites – the sheer number of social media sites and applications from LinkedIn to Snapchat means that almost everyone's tastes are catered for. If you prefer checking what your friends are doing and vice versa then Facebook and Twitter are obvious choices. If your taste is for a more professional and business oriented forum then LinkedIn will suffice. There are sites for teenagers all the way up to pensioners, that is the beauty of social media. Sites like Snapchat, Viber and Whatsapp make texting, photo and video sharing easy. They make you feel like you are close to your friends even though the proximity to one another may be hundreds or even thousands of miles. So whatever your taste there is a social media site online waiting for you.

Ease of use – whilst the possibilities with social media are endless the main point attracting increasing number of users is its simplicity and user friendly nature. The social media demographic spreads far and wide. Whether you are eight or eighty years of age the ease of use of the majority of social media sites makes accessibility high. An internet connection is needed, but after that once you have decided on the social media site you want to access setting up accounts is simple and for the internet security professionals amongst us, possibly too easy.

The dangers of social media

Hard to measure a return on investment (ROI) – whether an individual or company invests money in social media it is still difficult in 2015 to quantify a return on investment. You may invest money to generate new business or increase the hits on a company website. Investment may be done to promote a business or improve brand awareness. Specifying a monetary return candidly is hard. Companies may speculate that social media has benefited them and this may be true, but listing revenue from social media ventures on a profit and loss account is currently too hard to measure. With the improvement in analytical tools this may change but as it stands I doubt whether a business could confidently say how much they have made from social media investment.

What goes online stays online – the internet has changed the way we converse and communicate whether socially or professionally. The advent of social media has meant that our private lives are now more public than ever. The curious thing is we are not forced to set up an account on Facebook or Twitter yet we feel compelled to do so. The danger here is we use these sites and other social media sites as a forum to discuss and openly reveal information that should remain private.

As a lecturer in college once stated to me once any information is uploaded or added by us, it will stay on the internet forever. This is a scary thought. We may come home one Saturday morning intoxicated and decide to use social media to divulge personal information or worse we may write revealing information when sober. The addictive nature of social media means we can lose control of our ability to say stop when we know certain information should not be aired on public forums. Some sites will delete information if deemed inappropriate but social media sites are there ultimately to gather information about its users and in most cases sell this information on for profit. Deleted information simply moves to the background of sites and is kept hidden but it will not disappear. The more revealing one is about their personality or lives the better it is for the social media site owners. So the thing to remember is before revealing too much on social media, stop and think who may see this in the future. A prospective or current employer may find out you were holidaying in the Caribbean when you called in sick two years ago. My advice for you is to embrace social media, but always air on the side of caution and use sensibly. Inappropriate information posted ten or twenty years ago can come back to haunt you down the line.

Not using it at all – Ignorance, apathy, old age and even pure disinterest can prevent people utilising social media to its fullest. But to not use it all can be a damning indictment of a company's (or individuals) lack of foresight and knowledge of the potential that social media has to promote their business. Irish Prime Minister Enda Kenny's Twitter account as of late 2014 had been inactive for over three years. You may ask why set up an account if it's not going to be used. The prime minister is a very busy man but surely he has assistants and advisors who can direct him and his party's social media strategy. Not using Twitter for this length of time when other heads of state notably David Cameron (British Prime Minister) and Barack Obama (US President) are using it consistently doesn't look good and borders on embarrassing. David Cameron has tweeted about cabinet reshuffles thus airing information in real time. There is a suspicion that in late 2015 and early 2016 when the Irish government will be canvassing for re-election that all of a sudden social media accounts will become very active. Only time will tell here but for now a lack of use is curtailing the Irish governments reach and in particular its reach to social media users who tend to be a large percentage of the population.

Compliance – being overly compliant or not compliant at all can be a danger when using social media especially for businesses. Reputation is key for all businesses so a carefully thought out social media strategy is essential. If the strategy is not to engage with social media at all then in my opinion this approach is not sensible and will hold your business back. On the other hand a poorly thought out and delivered social media strategy can damage your business brand and customer base. The areas to consider when thinking about social media compliance are;

> *People* – Who will be involved and consulted in the process? Will it be a set group or will the whole company be surveyed and quizzed on their thoughts?

Branding – Will social media be used on company merchandise and promotional activities?

Training – Will staff be trained on how to engage with social media for the company's benefit?

Control – Who will control the social media policy? What can be posted and by whom? When can content be posted? Who will monitor the site and respond to customer queries? Is there an audit trail of content internally and externally? Should we use one mailbox or distribution network for social media?

Reputation – The most important aspect of any social media compliance policy is to make sure the company's reputation is protected. A loose policy could lead to reputational damage which may be hard to recover from. Once the four points above are adhered to a company's reputation should be safe from any unwanted damage.

The above points are listed as guidance when drafting up a social media compliance policy. Every company is different in its approach and extra care and attention may be needed in the development of a compliance policy surrounding use of social media. This will be at the discretion of individuals responsible for such policies.

Online bullying – traditional bullying can be described mostly as being physical and verbal in nature. The internet has changed all of this and in recent years cyber or online bullying has become more prevalent in our social lives. This unfortunately has translated into our professional and business lives. Most businesses have anti-bullying policies but the increase in cyber bullying has meant these policies need to incorporate strong measures to notice and punish online bullies in the workplace.

At its basic level emails can be used to exert power and potentially bully colleagues. The same can be said of social media. Employees can bully other employees using sites like Facebook, Snapchat, Whatsapp, Twitter and so on. Stringent, even draconian bullying policies need to be put in place in every company who engage with social media. These policies need to monitor potential bullying and enforce strict punishment for those found to have abused other colleagues inappropriately. There is no place for a bully in the office or online.

The social media do's and don'ts

Do

1. Use multimedia - use image and video based content wherever possible.

2. Add your social media or live feeds to your website or blog.

3. Use social media to build your personal brand and company brand.

4. Ask people to like, share, re-tweet, sign up for your newsletter and visit your website.

5. Support others - share appropriate comments, like their news feeds and support them in their endeavours. This is vital for success.

6. Give helpful, clever or inspiring content to your audience. The more you can provide value, the better your odds of ensuring your content is shared.

7. Embrace and engage with new social media websites and blogs. See where it takes you.

8. Use social media to gain a presence in your particular industry.

9. Save money by advertising and marketing via social media.

10. Do invest time in social media, it's free. Use new sites like www.slideshare.com

11. Do take social media seriously; it will enrich your business.

12. Do contact *www.thetalkingparrots.com* for all your anti-workplace bullying and social media consultancy needs. *thetalkingparrots.com* is a social media advisory and consultancy service owned by myself and it strives to help all businesses and individuals with their anti-workplace bullying and social media strategies. It is there to help any individual who is suffering from bullying at work with useful advice and tips given on how to cope in such stressful times. Please visit the website for further details.

Don't

1. Don't be offensive or post in poor taste.

2. Be aware of the mood you're in, don't post or tweet while angry.

3. Do not use social media as a forum to bully or cause harm to another individual.

4. Don't fail to acknowledge when people interact with you.

5. Do not act as a troll and cause deliberate harm to other social media sites and blogs.

6. Don't make spelling mistakes.

7. Don't assign your social media account entirely to an intern or an inexperienced colleague; this can be a recipe for disaster.

8. Don't get too familiar - you can be cordial without providing too much information. Respect your privacy and others.

9. Don't get into contentious or political conversations - if it's deemed to be contentious leave your response something along the lines of *'thank you for your comment, 'We will respond to it shortly'* or alternatively take the conversation offline, ask for a telephone number or email address to respond.

10. Keep it business related, know the lines between professional and non-professional.

11. Don't abuse your own name or that of your organization; reputation is vital for success.

12. Don't be scared of social media, it won't bite, once used correctly.

Eight companies who use social media positively

Many companies have taken social media engagement by the scruff of the neck and utilised its potential to benefit their respective companies. The eight companies below have developed a social media strategy to work for their business and the investment they have made is working. The list is not exhaustive and many other companies worldwide are currently using social media positively.

1.   Starbucks (*www.starbucks.ie*)

Starbucks is well renowned for its coffee worldwide but it doesn't rest on its laurels. It has used visual and image oriented sites such as Instagram to upload artistic photos of its coffee, some of which are taken by its customers. Its Twitter account is regularly active and has been used amongst other things to educate followers on its coffee, culture and brand. "*Tweet a Coffee*" is used to engage with followers, who want to share and comment on their experiences of Starbucks.

2. Boston Consulting Group (*www.bcg.com*)

Initially BCG was utilising the power of Facebook to communicate with its following and clientele but recently they have changed their social media strategy. Now the focus is on using Twitter and LinkedIn. They use LinkedIn to promote products to its following and audience, share other content and use it as a recruitment tool. Twitter is used to keep followers up to date on various activities and news going on in BCG and to interact with its followers who may have questions or comments to make. In tandem with using the main social media sites BCG also uses applications like Pulse which can aggregate specific data.

3. American Express (*www.americanexpress.com*)

American Express has been very creative in their use of social media. Firstly they use social media as a medium for enabling business by connecting members with millions of merchant partners. Card members can easily load merchant offers to their cards via hash-tags on Twitter and also they have the ability to tweet special hash-tags to make purchases. They have now partnered with the travel website TripAdvisor so customers can sync their cards to their TripAdvisor profiles and then upload special offers to their cards. These partnerships and innovative ideas have put American Express a step ahead of their competitors. They have not just used Twitter in the traditional sense; they have instead explored its market power and enticed users to follow them by offering niche product offers.

226

4.   Newcastle Brown Ale (*www.newcastlebrown.com*)

Newcastle Brown Ale has used social media platforms to do its advertising. It has ignored the traditional advertising campaigns used on television during big commercial events such as the Super Bowl. So by using social media it has saved itself a large amount of unnecessary extra spend. Using famous actresses like Anna Kendrick has proven useful as well helping campaigns go viral.

5.   Goldman Sachs (*www.goldmansachs.com*)

Traditionally financial institutions have tended to be careful about their activity on social media channels, and Goldman Sachs is no exception. The company doesn't delve too deeply into social media but instead uses a few sites like LinkedIn and YouTube carefully to advertise its financial products and keep customers up to date on the business. These updates can include information on employee profiles, financial advice and company news such as quarterly projected profits, important new hires and so on. LinkedIn can be used to advertise new positions and YouTube is used to upload videos on financial programs being undertaken and important economic news.

6. Capital One (*www.capitalone.com*)

This bank uses its Facebook and Twitter pages as a forum to discuss issues customers may have with the bank, whether positive or negative. The bank's policy is to respond to every post whether in the public forums of social media or privately. On Pinterest, Capital One has a few dozen boards dedicated to holiday campaigns and DIY crafts. The company has also taken advantage of the "*place pins*" feature by mapping out dream honeymoon spots. These ideas generate interest in the bank and therefore become marketing tools with the hope that customers take up loans for holiday, home improvements and so on.

7. Whole Foods Market (*www.wholefoodsmarket.com,*

www.wholefoods.ie)

Whole Foods specialise in healthy option foods and have over 500 stores worldwide including Dublin, Glasgow, Canada and the USA. They began training its employees in social media at a local shop level to help stores directly respond to customer service queries. This meant customers were getting a sense of community and felt a personal connection to their local stores. The social media platforms were dealing with local clientele. When a company is as big as Whole Foods Market, showing a local touch might not make great business sense, but it does resonate positively amongst local shoppers. Whole Foods also used social media in 2013 to educate shoppers on genetically modified foods (GMOs). Facebook and Twitter were used to answer customer questions and provide feedback on GMOs.

8. Southwest Airlines (*www.southwest.com*)

Southwest Airlines is a prime example of a company that has a focused social media strategy which incorporates the following sites, Twitter, Facebook, Pinterest, Instagram, YouTube, and Flickr. They use the sites to upload videos, vintage photos, travel tips, and customer service interactions. The company's reputation for social media usage is strong amongst its following. In 2013 it was named number seven on *Fortune*'s World's Most Admired Companies for its ability to win over customer loyalty through using social media.

Are we too consumed with social media?

The answer simply is yes. As a society we are increasingly spending more and more of our time using social media. The reason primarily is that with the advent of enhanced technologies such as smart-phones, tablets, portable laptops and other gadgets, the ease at which we can access these sites is a problem. Our sleep patterns may even be disrupted with the constant thinking and pondering over certain social media sites. I know I spend too much time on social media sites, my excuse is my love for it and also my business interests but even when I factor in these excuses my usage is still too high. Hours on end can be lost every day with the endless trawling through of worthless information. The key is to spend your time intelligently on social media, accessing its full potential and delving into its untapped resources. For example LinkedIn can be a enriching and enlightening site for the professional, but whilst many a good article is posted on the site, a lot of rubbish is also uploaded.

I'm sure I am no different to the average thirty something, twenty something or most other age groups and demographics. The addictive nature and ease of use of social media means usage will only increase. For modern businesses who know they need to engage more in social media but are afraid of doing so, potential over usage by employees may be hindering their adaptation to social media sites. If they deem that employees' work will be disrupted by unnecessary social media usage then they might see this as a barrier to adaptation. But this barrier can be easily solved by limiting social media usage to certain trusted employees or to lunch hours. Abusing the privilege given can result in their access being blocked. Having a total blockage for no justifiable reason is in my opinion a poor social media strategy and not forward thinking. Whilst our personal usage probably needs to be curtailed or reduced, the need for business and corporations to engage needs to increase. That is the conundrum society and business faces.

Survey on social media usage

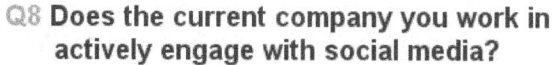

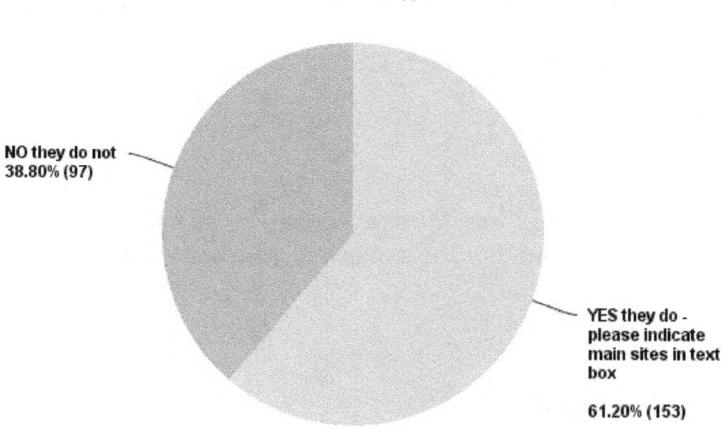

Q8 **Does the current company you work in actively engage with social media?**

Answered: 250   Skipped: 0

NO they do not
38.80% (97)

YES they do -
please indicate
main sites in text
box

61.20% (153)

This question was asked so that I could get an idea of how many companies use social media to advertise and promote their business. Just short of two thirds of the respondents stated the company they work for engage with social media and slightly over one third don't. This result surprised me a little. I didn't think considering that the majority of respondents worked in Ireland that the companies they worked for would engage with social media as much. But the reality is a lot of respondents work for indigenous companies, multinationals and foreign owned companies. So when this is

231

factored in the result is realistic and proof that companies are beginning to utilise the vast capabilities of social media.

Respondents also mentioned in the comments section that Facebook, Twitter and LinkedIn were the main sites their companies used. YouTube, Google+, Pinterest, Instagram and Yammer got honourable mentions but to a lesser degree.

Q9 Are employees allowed to use social media in the company you work in?

Answered: 250   Skipped: 0

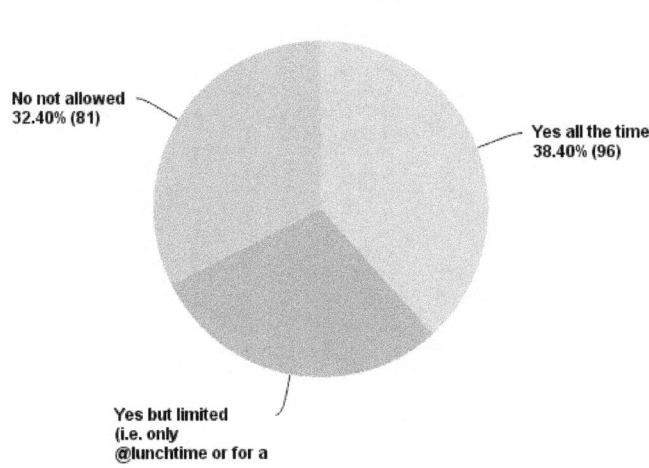

No not allowed
32.40% (81)

Yes all the time
38.40% (96)

Yes but limited
(i.e. only
@lunchtime or for a

From my own experience of working in various companies access to social media platforms has been generally restricted or banned totally. Whilst companies may argue it is unprofessional to spend time scanning through social media sites during work hours, the same can be said for the general use of the internet as well. These activities can distract employees and reduce their productivity. But a total ban is unreasonable and employees in my opinion should have access to some social media sites once they don't abuse the privilege and are conscious of upholding their companies' reputation at all times.

My question above asked simply if the companies the respondents worked in let them use social media platforms. If you take the answers to option two and three then it can be seen that the majority of companies frown upon usage with one third banning it totally. Limited access could mean a variety of things, possibly access during lunch or before 9am and after 5pm, but it does show that roughly a third of respondents companies are cautious with giving employees full access.

Then on the other hand a little over one third of respondents stated that the company they work in gives unlimited access to social media sites. I presume if this access is abused it is then revoked. From my own experience of working in deadline driven businesses, the time left for internet browsing is minimal so for the companies I worked for whether full or limited access was given, it didn't really matter. My guess is companies ban social media use during work because of the compliance risk associated with mis-use. This may be an ultra cautious approach but understandable at one level.

Q10 Have you ever been bullied whilst using a social media site?

Answered: 250   Skipped: 0

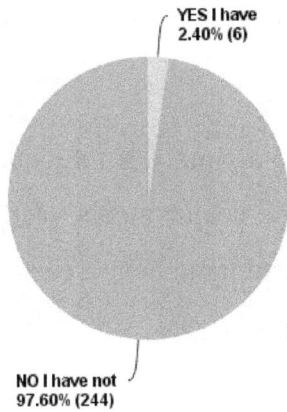

YES I have
2.40% (6)

NO I have not
97.60% (244)

Chapter three discussed bullying in the office and my own personal experiences with it. But there are many different forms of bullying and cyber bullying is one that has grown in prevalence since the inception of social media. It's the silent and secretive form of bullying that can cause catastrophic damage to the well being and mental health of its victims. My question above asked whether any of the respondents had experienced cyber bullying whilst using social media at work. Interestingly only 6 out of 250 respondents said they had. This was a little surprising as I thought the number would be higher. I am happy that the number admitting to cyber bullying is very low but I am not naive to think that this is the true number. Not all victims admit to have been bullied. Some are unsure if they are victims when the reality is they have been bullied or are being bullied. Unfortunately cyber bullying is a real danger but administrators of social media sites are becoming more aware of this threat now. Unfortunately it isn't a phenomenon that will ever fully disappear but on the evidence of this survey only a small percentage have been the victims of social media bullying during work which is positive if not perfect.

The future for social media

Irish companies in general have been slow to embrace the full potential of social media. The financial sector stands out for its apathy and apparent disillusionment with how to use the various social media platforms that are now available to market and advertise their brand and products. As illustrated in the previous section American companies seem to have grasped the social media concept better and are making full use of the tools available to them. It appears that the issue of privacy for Irish and European based companies is bigger than their American counterparts.

So what will social media become in the years ahead? There is no crystal ball here and speculating on where social media will be in ten or even five years is at best guesswork. The easy answer is that more people will use social media. The numbers who use Facebook continue to grow and other new platforms like Vine and Slideshare are slowly beginning to catch up in terms of usage. Nearly everyone in Ireland has a social media account with recent estimates putting this at 94%. Facebook is the market leader with Twitter second. When companies' realise what Twitter can do for their brand regarding market impact and coverage then Twitter may get close to Facebook in usage. Investment will be needed and a strong social media strategy is necessary for this to happen. The problem Twitter has encountered recently is bad publicity regarding the safety of the site and the propensity for certain individuals to use it as a forum to attack, abuse and threaten other individuals. The numbers worldwide who use Twitter is falling with no apparent growth foreseen in the near future. Creativity by the owners and increased confidence by the users and public is needed for growth to start again.

Certain trends do appear year on year and these trends can lay the foundation for what users and companies will be doing on social media in the short to medium term.

Investment will increase – Duke University in America published a study on social media in 2014 that showed most companies spent in and around nine per cent of their marketing budget on social media with this forecasted to increase to twenty five per cent by 2020. The numbers on the face of it seem small but for companies to be potentially spending a quarter of their entire marketing budgets on social media in five years is a staggering endorsement of the potential companies albeit primarily American companies are seeing in social media. A problem that the survey identified was that it was difficult for companies to measure or show the impact social media was having on their business. Historically since the inception of social media this has been an ongoing issue.

The cost of social media is no longer free – to set up a social media account with the majority of providers is free. After that it is down to the individual or company to spend what they want on their social media budget. The landscape is changing and companies like Facebook are changing the playing field in order to generate extra revenue. In 2015 and beyond using Facebook efficiently will cost more. Facebook is now encouraging its users to use its paid social ads offering which will reach a far greater percentage of fans than its traditional "*like*" button on a Facebook page.

PR firm Ogilvy in its recent research showed that only six per cent of posts by companies are seen by the companies or individuals who have liked their Facebook page. This reach is very small and most likely a reality check for Facebook users. Whilst Facebook methods might be sneaky and a little unethical, it is a business that needs to make money. After all it is listed on NYSE so technically shareholders need to be looked after. Higher profits, solid reputation and good sentiment equals higher stock price. So for companies to increase the true value that Facebook can provide, extra spending is essential. Methods employed by Facebook will inevitably see companies diversify in their social media usage to platforms like Instagram, Pinterest, Vine, Slideshare and new offerings like China's WeChat will become more popular.

Using tools to analyse if Tweets and Posts can drive sales - Google analytics has been around for a few years now. It can determine the visits and clicks to your website. This in turn can tell the company how many people are visiting the site and at what time. This then gives companies a tool to focus their attention at particular markets and advertise more in particular time periods. If website traffic is heaviest between 7 and 10pm at night when people are home from work, then extra attention needs to be focused on this time slot. Sounds simple doesn't it. Google Adwords is another service provided by Google where you can pay a premium to have particular words associated with your website appear higher up a search conducted by customers. This is referred to as SEO or search engine optimisation.

If Google Analytics can be combined with tools that show which social media platforms drive the most traffic and clicks (see Hootsuite, Brandwatch, 33Across, Salesforce's Marketing Cloud, to name but a few) then tweets and posts can be linked to sales levels. At its simplest, traffic levels on websites and social media sites dictate sales. Pinpointing this information is crucial. Once this happens sales levels can be given a true monetary value.

A new banking revolution is coming – Facebook has over one billion users worldwide and this number is growing. So roughly this accounts for between fourteen and seventeen per cent of the world's population. To have access to these individuals and their data is frightening, not only for the normal Facebook user but also for the banking industry. You may ask why? Traditionally personal banking has been done in either commercial or private banks. Facebook and other social media platforms have now the capacity to compete with these banks. Competing with day to day banking such as deposit and current (checking) accounts is unrealistic as regulating for this in each jurisdiction would be a logistical nightmare, too costly and impractical. But targeting credit and debit card payments, money transfers and other financial transactions may not be as difficult.

Recently in late 2014 Snapchat launched Snapcash, a product that enables users to transfer money to one another in the form of messages. It uses debit card information and is currently free. Facebook's Messenger Application has the capacity to do the same, and they announced in March 2015 that this option was being introduced. The threat is real for banks, credit card companies and money transfer providers (such as Western Union) as social media delves into the financial service world. Facebook's Messenger app has approximately 500 million users; this is less than the main site but a phenomenal user base. Merchants who want to use social media platforms to trade with will see this as a less expensive option. Current credit card companies charge between two and four per cent per transaction, this dilutes the profit made by traders. If social media platforms decide to compete in this market, credit card companies and money lenders will need to become more creative and innovative to survive. The likelihood is that in 2015 and beyond social media companies will be competing against each other for customers' money transactions, not just the traditional high street banks and credit card companies. Time will only answer this. The potential for buying goods on social media sites like Facebook is available and the company may enter the retail market as well in 2015 and beyond.

Forum for enhanced customer service – traditionally when an irate customer had a grievance, a phone call, email or letter could be sent to the company. It was too easy for companies to brush these grievances under the carpet and dismiss them. The beauty of social media is its reach. If you air a grievance on social media thousands, potentially millions will see it. The reputation and brand image of companies can be at risk if complaints are not handled properly. Many airline and internet providers have used social media to communicate directly with customers. The satisfaction levels amongst its clientele have increased due to the use of social media.

Not every company likes to air its dirty laundry in public so some companies will ask for conversations to be taken off social media and conducted in private via email or phone. There can be good reason for this; it's hard to communicate fully using Twitter as the character limits on tweets impacts on what can be said. Also certain data and information is confidential and cannot be divulged in public via social media. If a conversation becomes personal and abusive taking it off Facebook or Twitter is essential. To solve the problem noted above companies can tweet or post custom built codes and links that will lead to a unique phone number. If the aggrieved customer rings this number the problem can then be resolved with a company representative. When the conversation ends the number is deactivated and cannot be used again meaning the dialogue is protected. The power social media gives the customer is that a grievance cannot be ignored. Companies cannot afford to let grievances fester; social media reach is far too big for this happen.

Social media needs to be more creative – Facebook is the market leader but the power it exerts is diminishing. Other social media sites like Google+ have struggled to compete but their growing number of users does show that their group and community oriented focus is beginning to reap some dividends. They haven't tried to compete head on with Facebook as this strategy would be foolhardy, but instead tried to make users interact in group formats than on an individual basis. This innovative and creative thinking is what social media companies need to do if they are to survive. Social media is beginning to become more specialised and niche interest based, with sites such as Foodie a prime example, a site dedicated to cooks and food enthusiasts.

There is no such thing as privacy – to think we live in a world where our lives can be fully private is unrealistic. The internet has simply made this impossible. Once we upload data whether this is by video, image or text to the internet, it will always be in public view. Even if social media companies decide to delete the information held about its users it will still be locked away in the background of the sites and will not be fully destroyed. When we engage with social media sites we are unwittingly signing away elements of our private lives, parts that we may never get back. Sites like Snapchat and Secret Whisper claim to be private sites where all data is kept in house and not available to non-members. This unfortunately is not the case. Snapchat has been hacked repeatedly with sensitive data disappearing and user photos have been viewed by individuals that may have sinister motives. As mentioned above real anonymity and privacy on the internet is extremely difficult to achieve. This will not stop users trying to achieve privacy. The demand for this will grow exponentially. If you want to find out what information a social media company holds about you, you can simply request this directly. Be warned you may be shocked by the data companies like Facebook have. If you have downloaded the Facebook app on to your smart-phone, (or any social media app for that matter), then the company can in theory log and track your every movement. This information can then be stored and added to other sensitive data they may have regarding you. Potentially a scary thought for some readers and maybe something you are not aware of.

Facebook have introduced a new forum that will allow member interaction with each other without the necessity to reveal your name or location, called chat app rooms. This will focus around users with shared interests creating chat rooms. Facebook also supports Tor, an open-source anonymising service that is popular with journalists, politically sensitive individuals and law enforcers. Tor does have disadvantages as it can anonymise criminals' engaged in activities such as human trafficking, child abuse and other heinous illegal activities.

About the Author

David Malone is married with two children and lives in Dublin, Ireland. He holds a Masters Degree in Digital Innovation from the Michael Smurfit School of Business (University College Dublin) and also a Degree in Business Management from the Tallaght Institute of Technology in Dublin.

He has worked in the financial services industry for thirteen years with primary experience gained in Pensions and Financial Reporting. He currently works in the Insurance sector and is also the owner of the anti-workplace bullying and social media online consultancy business, *thetalkingparrots.com*. This is his first published book.

If you wish to contact David for any of your business needs he is available via LinkedIn, email and phone 087 6617335.